THE SIEGE OF LEXINGTON MISSOURI

The Battle of the Hemp Bales

LARRY WOOD

Charleston   London

THE
History
PRESS

Published by The History Press
Charleston, SC 29403
www.historypress.net

Cover image: "Battle of the Hemp Bales," by Dale Gallon. www.gallon.com.

First published 2014

Manufactured in the United States

ISBN 978.1.62619.536.3

Library of Congress CIP data applied for.

Notice: The information in this book is true and complete to the best of our knowledge. It is offered without guarantee on the part of the author or The History Press. The author and The History Press disclaim all liability in connection with the use of this book.

CONTENTS

ACKNOWLEDGEMENTS

I want to thank a number of people who contributed to making this book a reality, and I'd like to start with fellow Civil War historian James McGhee because it was he who encouraged me to write the book in the first place. In addition, he supplied a list of suggested sources and even provided transcribed copies of some of those sources. Finally, he read a first draft of the manuscript and provided valuable comments.

I need to thank Janae Fuller, administrator of the Battle of Lexington State Historic Site, for her help and cooperation during my several visits and numerous phone calls to the site, and she also supplied several photos for the book. I also want to thank John Maki, groundskeeper at the state historic site, for showing me around Lexington and pointing out the various places of interest related to the battle. In addition, John answered a number of my questions, particularly those pertaining to the battleground, and he, too, provided several photos. John also served as an early reader of the manuscript.

As usual, much of my research for this project was done via interlibrary loan, and I want to thank the reference staff at the Joplin Public Library, especially Patty Crane and Jason Sullivan, for cheerfully filling my interlibrary loan requests.

I made several trips to the Hulston Library and Museum at the Wilson's Creek Battlefield National Park, and I need to thank librarian Jeff Patrick and museum technician Alan Chilton for helping me with my research during those trips. In addition, I want to express my appreciation to museum curator Deborah Wood for supplying numerous images for this book.

ACKNOWLEDGEMENTS

I also made a couple trips to the Springfield–Greene County Library, and I want to thank local history librarians Patti Hobbs and Michael Price for their help during those visits.

During my visit to the Missouri Southern University Library, Penny Richeson of the audio-visual department and archivist Charles Nodler were very helpful.

Thanks to the staff at the State Historical Society of Missouri, especially to Laura Jolley for her help during my visit to the organization's research library in Columbia. Thanks also to Beth Lane and LeAnn Arndt of the society's Rolla branch for arranging for me to research some of the society's collections at the Missouri State University (MSU) Library in Springfield. Thanks, too, to Nathan Neuschwander and Sue Reichling for their help during my visit to the Music and Media Collections of the MSU Library.

Thanks also to Steve Mitchell and Robyn Burnett for their help during my visit to the Missouri State Archives in Jefferson City.

I want to thank Molly Kodner and Jaime Bourassa, associate archivists at the Missouri Historical Museum. Ms. Kodner responded to several research requests that I made via e-mail, and Ms. Bourassa supplied several photos from the museum's collection.

Thanks to Doug Gifford for furnishing me a copy of the John Taylor narrative, of which I had been unaware until I read his *Lexington Battlefield Guide*.

Joe Maghe kindly provided me with photos of several pertinent items from his Civil War collection.

Thanks to my wife, Gigi, for serving as a proofreader of the manuscript, for her help preparing some of the illustrations, and for her continued support.

Lastly, I need to thank Adam Ferrell, editorial director of The History Press, and Jaime Muehl, editorial department manager of The History Press, for her excellent edit of the manuscript. The book is more polished because of her professional attention to detail.

Chapter 1

LEXINGTON

Early 1861

O n the eve of the Civil War, Lexington, Missouri, was the fifth-largest town in the state with a population of over four thousand people, and it was the most important trading center on the Missouri River between St. Louis and Kansas City. Lexington was a commercial hub for the surrounding agricultural region, where wealthy, slaveholding planters reaped large profits from growing hemp, tobacco, and other products. Warehouses and factories lined the riverfront, and the town boasted three colleges, two newspapers, eight churches, and numerous thriving businesses.[1]

However, the town's sense of prosperity and tranquility was interrupted, as it was in the rest of the nation, by rumblings of war in the early months of 1861. Susan Arnold McCausland, a twenty-one-year-old newlywed living in Lexington at the time, recalled years later, "It was war time in the land, and Missouri was feeling the stir of the situation throughout all her bounds. In the little town of Lexington on the river there was…an eager impulse toward matters military, without however, any pronounced feeling of taking the side of either the North or South."[2]

Susan McCausland's memory of the situation in Lexington reflected Missouri's position of "armed neutrality," which meant that it would support the Union as long as Federal troops stayed out of Missouri and did not try to coerce the seceding states. Outgoing governor Robert M. Stewart had advocated such a position in late 1860, and incoming governor Claiborne F. Jackson had embraced it, at least nominally, when he took office in early 1861. A

Claiborne F. Jackson, Missouri's Confederate-allied governor. *Claiborne Jackson, #11499, in the collection of Wilson's Creek National Battlefield. Courtesy of the National Park Service.*

small but vocal minority of the state's citizens, concentrated in various rural areas, advocated immediate secession, and a similarly small but adamant group, led by a large German population in and around St. Louis, was made up of unconditional Unionists. However, the large majority of citizens were conditional Unionists who favored the position of armed neutrality, and a state convention called to consider the question of secession had voted overwhelmingly in March to stay in the Union, even though Missouri was a slaveholding state.[3]

Describing the same disposition toward neutrality that Susan McCausland recalled, the author of the 1881 *History of Lafayette County* said that the first military company raised in Lexington during the early days of 1861 was "composed of men of all shades of political opinion, the most of whom were of mature years." The county history said the first company was commanded by Captain John Tyler, who later entered the Union army, but Mrs. McCausland remembered that her father, Major E.G. Arnold, who was a graduate of the Virginia Military Institute, and Captain George Wilson, a West Point graduate and former officer in the U.S. Army, also led drills on "the wide and beautiful campus of the old Masonic College." In any case, the companies formed during the early months of 1861 were intended merely for home protection and to enforce Missouri's policy of armed neutrality. These "half-play companies," as Susan McCausland called them, favored neither the North nor the South but instead sought merely to maintain peace and to protect Lafayette County citizens from invasion by any outside force.[4]

However, when Confederates in South Carolina attacked Fort Sumter on April 12, the cannons of Charleston Harbor echoed across the nation, and Missouri's fragile façade of neutrality cracked. Although many Missourians still held out hope that their state could stay out of the looming war, some began to take sides. When Virginia seceded from the Union five days after the firing on Fort Sumter, for instance, Susan McCausland, a native of the Old Dominion, immediately hoisted a Confederate flag on a pole in her father's front yard at Broadway and Third Street in Lexington.[5]

Others around Lexington and throughout the state began to show their true colors as well. Despite Missouri's ostensible efforts at neutrality, Southern sentiment was strong throughout much of the state

Lexington resident Susan McCausland, a daring young woman of Southern sympathies during the Civil War, as she appeared in later life. *Courtesy of the Battle of Lexington State Historic Site.*

because most Missouri settlers had come from the upper tier of Southern states. This was especially true of Lafayette County, which had the largest slave population of all Missouri counties. As the county history noted, "The secessionists—or at least the conditional secessionists—were not only in the majority, but were bold, defiant, and aggressive."[6]

Asserting themselves on April 20, 1861, a group of Southern sympathizers from Lafayette and other counties of west-central Missouri seized the Federal arsenal at Liberty, and Hiram M. Bledsoe and Curtis O. Wallace of Lexington, who were among the group, brought two six-pound cannons captured at the arsenal back to Lexington. Then, on April 29, a group of Southern sympathizers petitioned the Lafayette County Court to appropriate funds for arming and equipping at least one thousand men, but the court declined to do so until the state legislature passed an act authorizing such action.[7]

Lafayette County, mainly because of its sizeable German population, was not without its active Union supporters as well. Although the outspoken Union men in the town of Lexington at the time numbered, according to the county history, no more than twenty or so, nearly all of them attended an organizational meeting at the courthouse on May 3, 1861. A contingent from the local Turner Society, a German athletic club that was also social and political in nature, filed in and raised a U.S. flag on the stage. The meeting was just getting started when a belligerent group of about fifty Southern sympathizers gathered outside the courthouse, led by "one Charles Martin," who, according to the county history, was "a man of desperate character."[8]

Nicholas Haerle, a Lexington saloonkeeper among the Turner group, remembered what happened next: "The speaker began and all at once there was a terrible noise outside, scolding, cursing and shouting. The lights in the hall were

Nicholas Haerle was run out of Lexington in the spring of 1861 because of his strong Union proclivity. *Courtesy of the Battle of Lexington State Historic Site.*

extinguished and only a candle burned where we sat. Then suddenly a wild gang came streaming into the hall, up to the stage and tore down our flag."[9]

As the group began marching out of the courthouse with the flag, Haerle got up and tried to wrest the banner away from the unruly horde. During the ensuing struggle, Martin shot Haerle in the leg, but the latter clung to the flag and fought his way through the mob toward the door, where, according to Haerle, he "got two blows on the head that knocked me in a stupor."[10]

Haerle was taken home and treated by a doctor, but he had barely gotten his wound bandaged when a party of armed men barged into his room. One of them, according to the injured man, took a paper out of his pocket and read the following decree: "In the name of the South Confederation and President Davis, we command you to leave town in twelve hours. If we find you in our town after this time, we will hang you on the next tree."[11]

Mrs. Haerle protested that the men should be ashamed for driving a man out of town who had never insulted anybody and only had done his duty as a citizen, especially since he was wounded, but the throng of men were deaf to her entreaties and repeated, as they marched away, that her husband must go. After packing a few necessities and making other hasty preparations, Haerle departed on a ferry boat at four o'clock the next morning, leaving his family behind in Lexington, although they were reunited in St. Louis a few weeks later.[12]

On May 10, 1861, about seven hundred state militiamen, who had gathered for routine training at Camp Jackson near the Federal arsenal in St. Louis, were arrested because Captain Nathaniel Lyon, commanding the arsenal, thought they meant to seize it for the Southern cause. As Federal troops marched the militiamen as prisoners through the streets of St. Louis, the troops were met by angry pro-Southern demonstrators taunting them and pelting them with rocks. When an unruly drunk among the demonstrators tried to force his way through the Federal troops and was pushed away, he fired a shot that wounded a Federal officer. As the confrontation continued to escalate, the Federal soldiers rashly opened fire on the civilian protestors, killing almost thirty of them, including at least one woman and one child.[13]

The Camp Jackson affair infuriated people throughout Missouri, including not just Southern sympathizers but also citizens who had previously considered themselves conditional Unionists. If the firing on Fort Sumter and the resultant war between the Union and the Confederacy had cracked Missouri's façade of neutrality, the Camp Jackson affair shattered it. In fact, the incident so aroused the people of the state that, had the vote on secession been taken after May 11, Missouri might well have joined the Confederacy.

As Susan McCausland recalled, "This act set the State in a flame of feeling, with the result that an immediate alignment was made for one side or the other about to enter upon the great modern tragedy of the war between the States." In Lexington, the overwhelming but tentative Southern sentiment of the townspeople from earlier in the year now exploded into open rebellion. "Small Confederate flags began to be displayed from private residences," said Mrs. McCausland, "and the old flag was set afloat to the winds from all public buildings of the town."[14]

After Camp Jackson, Governor Jackson quickly got a "Military Bill," which he had previously advocated, passed through the state legislature disbanding the old militia and establishing the Missouri State Guard to resist any attempt of the Federal army to "invade" Missouri. Former governor and Mexican War veteran Sterling Price was appointed general in command of the newly formed state force, and nine military divisions, representing nine different sections of the state, were created.

Despite the inflamed passions caused by the Camp Jackson affair, Price and others still sought to maintain Missouri's neutrality and to keep the war out of the state, and he and General William S. Harney, commanding the U.S. Army's Department of the West, signed an agreement to that effect on May 21, 1861. However, Missouri congressman and unconditional Unionist Francis P. Blair Jr. influenced President Lincoln to replace Harney with the more militant Lyon, who was skeptical of his predecessor's agreement with Price. Governor Jackson and General Price met with Lyon, who had been promoted to brigadier general, at the Planters Hotel in St. Louis on June 11 in an effort to continue the terms of the agreement. Jackson and Price agreed to disband the Missouri State Guard and maintain the peace if Lyon would agree to keep Federal forces out of the state, but the fiery Lyon refused to bargain and essentially declared war on Missouri.[15]

Jackson, Price, and their escort retreated to the state capital at Jefferson City, burning bridges and destroying telegraph lines along the way. On June 12, Jackson issued a proclamation calling for fifty thousand volunteers to enroll in the Missouri State Guard, and he ordered its commanders to concentrate their forces at Boonville and Lexington. Abandoning Jefferson City and taking a portion of the state troops already assembled, he then moved the seat of state government to Boonville, while Price headed to Lexington to set up a recruiting and training camp there.

Pursuing Jackson and Price, General Lyon arrived at Jefferson City on June 15 and found the state capital abandoned. Accompanied by about 1,700 Union soldiers, he resumed the chase and reached Boonville on June

Right: Union general William S. Harney, commander of the Department of the West, with whom General Price forged an agreement in May 1861 to try to keep the Civil War out of Missouri. *General Wm. S. Harney, #31803, in the collection of Wilson's Creek National Battlefield. Courtesy of the National Park Service.*

Below: Planters Hotel in St. Louis, where Governor Jackson and General Price met with General Nathaniel Lyon to try to reach a compromise and preserve peace in Missouri. *Missouri History Museum, St. Louis.*

Northern political cartoon portraying General Lyon's defeat of Governor Jackson and General Price's Missouri State Guard forces at the Battle of Boonville. *Courtesy of the Library of Congress.*

17, where he put to flight several hundred of Jackson's raw state troops. Most of the routed state troops hightailed it to Lexington, while Jackson himself started toward southern Missouri via Warsaw, accompanied by Brigadier General Mosby M. Parsons's Sixth Division, which had arrived too late to take part in the so-called Boonville Races.[16]

Meanwhile, new recruits for the fledgling Missouri State Guard poured into Lexington from all over the western and northern parts of the state. Among the early arrivals was Salem H. Ford, who, in answer to Governor Jackson's call for volunteers, left his home at Parkville and marched with a group of other men from Platte County to Lexington. "We found there about two thousand men ready to buckle on their armor in defense of the South," Ford remembered years later. "Some were armed with shotguns, squirrel rifles, and the majority of them were unarmed." Ford was appointed orderly sergeant of a company in the newly organized regiment of Colonel John T. Hughes.[17]

Andrew McGregor, one of the recruits who fled to Lexington after being at the Boonville skirmish, also remembered the poorly armed and poorly equipped condition of the fledgling army he had joined. "We had no ammunition; shotguns and squirrel guns were our arms. We had no artillery, no food, no clothes to speak of, and had no source of supply beyond what we had gathered up to this time." By the time McGregor reached Lexington, the number of recruits there had swelled to almost eight thousand, according to his guess. General Lyon, however, estimated the strength of the Missouri State Guard at five or six thousand, and McGregor admitted that, while still in camp at Lexington, some of his company became dissatisfied and went back home.[18]

Not all the men who wanted to join the Missouri State Guard could reach Lexington. This was especially true of those north of the Missouri River. Brothers Caldwell and Sam Dunlap were among a party of about forty young men from Buchanan County who left home in mid-June bound for Price's recruiting camp. At Liberty in Clay County, Caldwell and Sam were captured, required to take an oath of allegiance to the United States, and then released on the condition that they return home and not take up arms against the Federal government.[19]

Ephraim Anderson, who was camped in Randolph County in the days after the Boonville skirmish awaiting an opportunity to cross the river, managed to elude capture, but he had to postpone his plans to join Jackson's state forces. "The Federals had taken possession of all the ferries on the river," he later recalled, "destroying some of the boats, and guarding vigilantly those that continued to run; even the flats and skiffs had been gathered up, and shared the same fate. The men on this side who desired to go to the army, found it almost impossible to cross, and did not attempt it in large bodies. Everything of this kind was done in a very quiet manner. The country soon swarmed with soldiers, who were hunting up and capturing the boys that had been to Booneville."[20]

Would-be recruits south of the river also had to deal with Union forces. During the second week of June, Edmund B. Holloway, who had recently resigned his captain's commission in the U.S. Army and accepted a colonel's commission from Governor Jackson, was camped on Rock Creek in present-day Independence with about three hundred Missouri State Guard recruits from Jackson County and the surrounding area, including some whom Holloway had sworn in at Lexington just days before. On June 13, Captain David S. Stanley marched out from Kansas City with about one or two hundred Federal troops, who had recently arrived from Fort Leavenworth, and came upon the Missouri State Guard training camp. Holloway and his aide rode out and met Stanley under a flag of truce, but Stanley began to retreat when he noticed a threatening flanking movement from the state troops. When Holloway, who was still wearing his Federal uniform, turned to wave his troops back, some of the edgy recruits, construing the motion as a signal from Stanley for his troops to attack, opened fire, killing their own colonel, as well as his aide.[21]

Susan McCausland watched with eager interest as raw farm boys streamed into her hometown to join the newly formed Missouri State Guard, and she, like Ford and McGregor, was struck by the inferior arms and equipment available to them. Years later, she recalled the new soldiers "buckling on…such accouterments of war as a hitherto peaceful people could muster from the country's store of bird guns, turkey and deer rifles, and such side arms as belong to times of peace."[22]

The anonymous author of the 1881 county history also remarked on the meager arms, saying that most of the first recruits who formed at Lexington to join the Missouri State Guard had only weapons that they were able to supply themselves. He remembered that some of the recruits had squirrel guns or double-barrel shotguns, and he also recalled, "A few sanguinary individuals had bowie knives."[23]

At first, Brigadier General James S. Rains, whose Eighth Military District covered almost all of western Missouri south of the Missouri River, was in charge of training and organizing the troops gathered at Lexington. Visiting the new recruits at their camps in Lexington, he "addressed them in an excellent speech," according to the county history. The Masonic College was chosen as the headquarters for the Southern troops, and the surrounding college property served as their training ground. The college was located on an elevation in the north part of Lexington near the Missouri River between the original town site, called Old Town, on the east and the current town site, called New Town, on the west. The three-story brick building had been erected in 1847 and dedicated the following year by the local Masonic lodge as a college for young men throughout the region, primarily orphaned children of deceased Masons. With the outbreak of the Civil War, however, it had been taken over for military purposes.[24]

Among the Missouri State Guard units organized at Lexington were a regiment under John T. Graves composed of Lafayette County men and an artillery battery that was also composed primarily of Lafayette County men. Hiram M. Bledsoe was made captain of the battery, and Curtis Wallace was first lieutenant. The battery consisted, at first, of only two guns, an iron six-pounder that had been cast at Morrison's foundry in Lexington and a nine-pounder that had been captured by American troops at the Battle of Sacramento during the Mexican War, donated to Missouri by the federal government, and then donated by the state to Lafayette County several years before the Civil War. Called Old Sacramento, or just Old Sac, it had been bored out to a twelve-pounder at Morrison's foundry. The two cannons Bledsoe and Wallace had taken from the arsenal at Liberty were abandoned as unusable, as was another six-pounder that had been cast at Morrison's foundry.[25]

Price, who had departed Boonville on June 16, arrived in Lexington on the eighteenth to find several thousand Missouri State Guard troops. He had scarcely begun their training and organization, however, when he learned of the fiasco at Boonville on the seventeenth, and he realized that a retreat to southwest Missouri was necessary so that he might find a suitable place to train and equip his raw army unmolested and also might enlist the protection and cooperation of Confederate general Ben McCulloch, who was somewhere near the Arkansas border. Turning command of the recruits back over to Rains, Price ordered Rains to move the troops in the direction of Lamar and to effect a junction with Governor Jackson and the rest of the Missouri State Guard. Meanwhile, with a small escort, Price hurried ahead to try to find McCulloch.[26]

On June 20, as the ragtag Missouri State Guard prepared to leave Lexington, "the ladies and citizens," according to the county history, "generally turned out to bid them adieu, to wave them fond farewells, and to pray for their success and safe return." Then the troops took up the line of march and "left Lexington for Dixie," as Andrew McGregor remembered the occasion. In less than three months, however, they would be back, a much different army than when they left.[27]

Chapter 2

LEXINGTON

Summer 1861

Following the action at Boonville, General Lyon's chase after Governor Jackson's retreating state troops was stalled for about two weeks because of heavy rains and difficulty in getting a supply train ready. Finally, in late June, Lyon ordered a regiment of Union reserve troops up the Missouri River to occupy Lexington while he and the bulk of his army belatedly started south.[1]

The Fifth Regiment, United States Reserve Corps, arrived at Lexington aboard the steamboat *White Cloud* on July 9. Composed largely of Germans, the regiment had been organized at St. Louis in May and enlisted for three months. Numbering slightly over one thousand, the regiment was commanded by Colonel Charles G. Stifel, who owned a brewery in St. Louis, and his men had been the main ones involved in the Camp Jackson affair. Many Southern sympathizers in Missouri had a particular dislike for Union soldiers of German descent, whom they contemptuously referred to as the "damn Dutch," and according to the 1881 *History of Lafayette County*, "the arrival of these, the first Federal troops, created no little commotion in Lexington. As they disembarked and marched up from the wharf the angry citizens of secession proclivities called to them and shouted at them in no very complimentary terms."[2]

Susan McCausland was one of the citizens who did not welcome the sight of the Federal troops, whom she remembered as "a regiment of foreigners, some of whom spoke English not at all." According to Susan, when the boat carrying the Federals first appeared, almost all the "Confederate

Colonel Charles G. Stifel, whose Union forces occupied
Lexington during the summer of 1861. *Missouri History Museum,
St. Louis.*

bunting" that Lexington residents had proudly flown in recent days was
quickly taken down. The only exception was the flag that she herself had
raised on her father's lawn at Third and Broadway almost two months
earlier. Broadway was the main road leading from the levee into town, and
as the Union soldiers marched up from the river, Susan and some other
women stood on her father's lawn beside the Southern flag watching the
soldiers' approach. As the troops came abreast of the Arnold home, a group
of them surrounded the women, demanding that they take down the flag.
Susan stubbornly refused and "found herself amazingly confronted by a

Susan McCausland's residence as it appears today. *Photo by the author.*

body of folk hostile and threatening, with guns and bayonets, who made threats to her as she stood upon her own ground."[3]

When one of the soldiers moved as if to take the offending flag from its staff, Susan ran over and took it into her own hands. Her husband, twenty-nine-year-old William McCausland, looked down the street from his dry goods store a block or two away and, seeing the commotion, came running to the scene with a shotgun in his hands to defend his wife's honor. Susan immediately dropped the flag, grasped William's hand, and lowered the barrel of the gun to save her rash husband from being shot. One of the soldiers picked up the flag and carried it away, while several others marched Susan's husband away as a prisoner of war. He and some other Southern sympathizers who were arrested shortly afterward were held as prisoners aboard the *White Cloud*, but most of them were later released on parole.[4]

On the same day that the Federal troops arrived, acting Lexington mayor R.M. Henderson sent a letter to Lieutenant Colonel Robert White, Stifel's second in command, asking him to meet with citizens at the courthouse that afternoon at four o'clock to "address them on the subject of your mission." The citizens might have mistakenly thought that White was in command, or more likely, they simply preferred to deal with him, since he was one of the few "American" officers among the regiment and probably one of the few who spoke English fluently. In fact, despite Colonel Stifel's superior rank, White considered himself in virtual command of the post because it was he who had met with Lyon at Boonville in late June and received the orders to occupy Lexington, while Stifel had only joined the expedition upon White's brief return to St. Louis for reinforcements. At any rate, White, without consulting Stifel first, agreed to meet with the citizens, and he told them they had nothing to fear and would be protected if they obeyed the law. The meeting, however, strained the already tense relationship between Stifel and White, as many of the German soldiers of the regiment felt that White had usurped Stifel's authority and position.[5]

Almost immediately upon their arrival in Lexington, Stifel's regiment took over the Masonic College and surrounding grounds, dubbed Camp Fremont, and began fortifying the place by digging entrenchments. When one company mutinied a few days later by playing cards and refusing to work, Colonel White gave them a "sharp lecture" and finally got them to go back to work.[6]

Meanwhile, scouting parties went out through the countryside, and a detachment was also sent up the river to destroy boats, thereby preventing Southern recruits from crossing to reinforce Price's army. In addition,

Masonic College. *Courtesy of the Battle of Lexington State Historic Site.*

the Federals confiscated about two hundred kegs of gunpowder, thirty-three muskets, one cannon, and other materials and supplies from in and around Lexington. The cannon was the six-pounder that had been cast at Morrison's foundry and then abandoned by the retreating Southern army. One of the two cannons brought to Lexington from the Liberty arsenal by Bledsoe and Wallace was also later confiscated and restored to service. Both guns eventually became part of the Lexington Home Guard Battery of C.M. Pirner.[7]

The citizens of Lexington continued to prefer dealing directly with Lieutenant Colonel White rather than with Colonel Stifel. On July 12, three days after the regiment's arrival, an anonymous local citizen sent a letter to Colonel White suggesting that fellow resident Silas Silver was a secessionist and that, if White would search the man's house and premises, he would find a store of hidden gunpowder and weapons.[8]

Other Federal units soon reinforced Stifel's regiment at the Lexington post. Captain Robert H. Graham's Illinois company of Independent Rangers came down from Leavenworth, and several other companies, drawn from Union men of the Lexington area, were organized and armed. One of the latter units was a company under Captain Frederick W. Becker, composed principally of Germans from Lafayette County's Freedom Township. Another was raised at Lexington, mostly from members of the Turner Society, and commanded at first by Gustave Pirner and later by Henry Emde. A third company was also organized at Lexington by Captain Frederick Neet, and a fourth company was commanded by Captain Richard Ridgell of Carroll County and made up of men from Carroll, Ray, and Lafayette Counties. Each of these companies had about fifty men.[9]

Becker was promoted to acting major and installed at the Masonic College in command of three of the local companies, while Stifel's men camped on the surrounding grounds and throughout the town. According to the county history, Becker's promotion brought out his pretentious side: "He had very little education, but affected a great deal of wisdom, and, dressed in a little authority, was given to many fantastic tricks. He wore a pair of huge epaulets and a stunning uniform; kept himself secluded from the common herd, was surrounded by a number of guards, and was as difficult of access as a czar." Still, the author of the county history allowed that Becker was a fair soldier who was knowledgeable of military tactics and who drilled his men with some skill.[10]

Colonel Stifel stayed in Lexington only about five days before departing for St. Louis to bring back additional supplies and ammunition, and Colonel

Colonel Robert White organized the
Fourteenth Missouri Home Guards at
Lexington during the summer of 1861.
Missouri History Museum, St. Louis.

White was glad to be left
in complete command at
Lexington. White felt that
Stifel was too lax, partly
because he was the owner
of a brewery and "nearly
every man in the regiment
was either (and many
both) a beer seller or a beer
drinker." White believed that
Stifel was, therefore, hesitant
to offend his customers, and he
saw the colonel's absence as an
opportunity to instill a little discipline in
what he considered a lax outfit. For instance,
in response to persistent rumors of Rebels in the area, even though White
did not believe the rumors, he assigned the men increased guard duty just
to acquaint them with what it was like. Had the rumors proved true, White
felt that any one hundred determined men "could have grabbed up and
whipped our whole force," which he said numbered five hundred.[11]

In late July, Stifel, having returned from St. Louis, got word of a camp of
Rebels on the river about six miles below Lexington, reportedly under the
command of Joseph O. Shelby, captain of a Missouri State Guard company
composed mostly of Lafayette County men. Shelby, a hemp grower and
paper manufacturer at Waverly before the war, had been south with
Governor Jackson and participated in the Battle of Carthage, but he was
now back in his home territory on a recruiting mission. A detachment of
Union soldiers under Colonel Stifel went out from Lexington by land, and a
detachment under White went down the river by boat to break up the camp.
White fired a howitzer from his boat into the woods where he thought the
Rebels were camped, and although he didn't know the result of the firing for
sure, he later heard that it had caused them to make a hasty retreat.[12]

Sometime after the arrival of Stifel's regiment on July 9, James S. Lightner, director of the Farmers' Bank of Missouri at Lexington, was taken prisoner and held on Colonel Stifel's boat. The county history seems to suggest that his arrest occurred shortly after Stifel's arrival, near the same time that William McCausland was taken prisoner. According to Lieutenant Colonel White's memoir, though, Lightner was arrested on July 29, close to the time of the Shelby incident. Lightner was supposedly taken prisoner because a party of Rebels under his charge was suspected of having fired at Colonel Stifel while he was out on a boat expedition, and two Union soldiers were killed and a couple of others seriously wounded in the incident. White remembered Lightner as "a bad man generally and a drunkard" and the "leader of a gang of desperadoes" who had been "causing mischief to the loyal people of Lafayette County." Considering Lightner's job as a prominent bank director, it seems more likely that he was arrested simply because he was a leading citizen of Lexington who also happened to be an outspoken Southern sympathizer and because Union authorities wanted to seize the assets of his bank.

What is known for sure is that on or about July 30, Lightner was killed by his guard, Henry Hoefel, reportedly while trying to escape. According to White and other Union sources, Lightner became quarrelsome and refused to obey the guard. Saying he was going to leave, he picked up a chair and made a move as if to attack Hoefel with it, forcing the guard to shoot him in self-defense. White also claimed that Lightner was drunk when he was arrested on the twenty-ninth, that he developed delirium tremors during the night, that Colonel Stifel dosed him with brandy to try to calm his nerves, and that the excessive alcohol is probably what made him belligerent.[13]

Southern sympathizers, however, were outraged by the killing and claimed it was nothing short of murder, or as White remembered it, Lightner's death caused "quite a commotion in Lexington and the counties surrounding." Some of the citizens of Lexington petitioned White that civil authorities be allowed to conduct an inquest on Lightner's body, but White refused, feeling that Lexington was under military authority at the time and not subject to civil authority. This decision angered many of the local people and turned some of those who had previously supported White against him.[14]

One of those disturbed by Lightner's killing was Jo Shelby. On July 30, he sent a letter to White complaining of the rumored killing and seeking confirmation. Shelby said he was holding thirteen Union men and that he wanted to treat them as prisoners of war but that "if our men, when captured, are to be shot, hanged, or otherwise deprived of life, I shall cause my prisoners to be dealt with accordingly." Shelby added that he was sending the letter by a Union man "should you not condescend to communicate with a <u>Rebel</u>, such as I am, such as I claim to be."[15]

Near the middle of August, Stifel's regiment made preparations to return to St. Louis to be mustered out of service, the term of their three-month enlistment having expired. On August 15, a group of Lexington citizens, worried about Stifel's imminent departure, sent a letter to General John C. Fremont, commanding the Department of the West at St. Louis, asking that he send reinforcements to Lexington. On the same day, a group of citizens

Joseph O. Shelby participated in the so-called First Siege of Lexington in late August 1861. *Joseph O. Shelby, #31493, in the collection of Wilson's Creek National Battlefield. Courtesy of the National Park Service.*

that ironically included accused secessionist Silas Silver petitioned White to "remain and take command of the troops here until some other suitable officer shall arrive."[16]

White had, in fact, been organizing his own regiment from the troops at Lexington that were not part of Stifel's command and from other men he had recruited. He had penciled himself in as the prospective colonel and Captain Graham as the prospective lieutenant colonel. However, he decided to return to St. Louis rather than complete the organization. He hoped that Graham would be left in command at Lexington, but Stifel instead chose Becker to command the post once the St. Louis regiment was gone. The choice irritated White, who considered Becker a "most unworthy being—drunken, reckless and I believe a coward."[17]

On or about August 15, Colonel Stifel's reserves left Lexington by steamboat headed back to St. Louis. The regiment, according to Colonel White, had accomplished no "brilliant achievement" but had done its duty by securing that part of Missouri for the Union. Near the beginning of the Federals' trip downriver, Shelby fired on the boat, reportedly wounding several men, but the steamer continued on without further incident. At Jefferson City, Colonel White left Stifel's regiment to attend to business and encountered Colonel Thomas A. Marshall, who was on his way to Lexington with the First Illinois Volunteer Cavalry. Encouraged by Colonel Marshall, White decided to go back to Lexington as well and complete the organization of his regiment.[18]

In late August, while Major Becker was in charge of the post at Lexington, Henry L. Routt, a lawyer from Clay County who had led the raid on the Liberty arsenal in April, surrounded the town of Lexington with a force of several hundred men and arrested some prominent Union men of the area, including former Missouri governor Austin A. King and former state supreme court judge John F. Ryland. During Routt's investment of the town, according to a contemporaneous report, "a good deal of skirmishing took place in the streets and in the woods on both sides of the river." Susan McCausland remembered that the Southerners "daily came dashing into town in small groups to give an exchange of shots and out again." In one of these "daring and useless exploits," as Susan called them, she saw a friend of hers named James Withrow unhorsed and mortally wounded by a bayonet-wielding Union soldier. All told, eight Southerners and one Union soldier were reported killed in the skirmishing.[19]

A lieutenant during the Mexican War and a veteran of the 1850s border wars between Missouri and Kansas, Routt had commanded a company in the Missouri State Guard at Carthage and Wilson's Creek, but now he was back in his home territory trying to raise a regiment and styling himself a colonel. He set up a camp on the fairgrounds about two miles south of Lexington, where he held the prisoners. Routt's force initially numbered about 800, including the command of Jo Shelby, who was also fresh from Wilson's Creek, but bolstered by new recruits, the force quickly ballooned to at least 1,200. A member of Routt's fledgling command later estimated the number at 2,000. On August 27, Routt sent a message to Becker under a flag of truce demanding the surrender of the post, but Becker flatly refused. He also declined Routt's proposal to exchange prisoners. The next day, Routt requested a conference, and Becker, Captain Graham, and Lieutenant Richard Brown came out about halfway between the fort and the fairgrounds to parley with Routt, Captain Shelby, and Colonel John W. Reid, Price's commissary general. Lieutenant Brown, the soldier who had struck down Susan McCausland's friend Withrow, later described Routt's command as "a motley crowd" that reminded him of "Falstaff's company of recruits as depicted in Shakespeare's play."[20]

Routt renewed his demand for an immediate surrender of the Lexington post, but it was again adamantly refused. Two days later, on August 30, the Rebel forces retired, having learned of the approach of a Federal force from the direction of Sedalia (Marshall's regiment). According to the county history, Routt's retreat was also hastened by the firing of three homemade shells from an old brass mortar by brothers Charles and Gustave Pirner, who had seen military service in Germany. This surrounding of the town by Routt's forces in late August was sometimes called a "siege" in contemporaneous reports, but events were about to unfold that would redefine what was meant by the "Siege of Lexington."[21]

On or about August 31, Lieutenant Colonel White arrived at Lexington by steamboat; took command of the post, which was renamed Fort White; and resumed the organization of his regiment. White, as acting colonel, promoted Graham to lieutenant colonel and replaced Becker with J.F. Tyler as major. The regiment, called the Fourteenth Missouri Home Guards Infantry, consisted of Graham's company, Emde's company (in which Becker was a first sergeant), Neet's company, Ridgell's company, and one or two other companies that had not been fully organized.[22]

A day or two later, Colonel Marshall reached Lexington with about five hundred men and relieved White of his brief command. The county history praised the Illinois regiment as "a fine body of men" but lamented that they were poorly armed."[23]

After leaving Lexington, Colonel Routt moved off to the west toward Independence. Colonel Reid, who, like Routt, had been an officer during the Mexican War and a participant in the border wars, started south, taking the prisoners with him. Meanwhile, Captain Shelby retired to "his old rendezvous on Tabo Creek," about eight miles east of Lexington. On September 1, Shelby wrote to Colonel White complaining about the arrest of a man named James Hicklin, who, according to Shelby, had been taken prisoner simply because Shelby's men had watered their horses on Hicklin's land. Shelby claimed Hicklin was not even home at the time his men watered their horses, and he said he was holding two of White's men pending the disposition of Hicklin's case. Shelby sent the letter to White by a Union man because he wasn't sure White was in command at Lexington. If he'd known for sure, he assured White, he would have allowed one of his own men to deliver the message, but he didn't trust the other Federal officers.[24]

On September 4, the Thirteenth Missouri Infantry under Colonel Everett Peabody and a battalion of U.S. reserves under Major Robert T. Van Horn arrived at Lexington by steamboat from Kansas City to reinforce

Marshall, and they camped on the fairgrounds. On September 7, Colonel Marshall seized the assets of the Farmers' Bank of Missouri at Lexington, per instructions from General Fremont, who had ordered that the funds of western Missouri banks be impounded or "secured" to prevent the money from being used to finance operations against the Federal government. The funds in the Farmers' Bank, of which James Lightner had been director, amounted to almost $1,000,000, including over $165,000 in gold. The same day, September 7, Peabody left for Warrensburg to seize the money of the banks there and, if possible, to form a junction with General Jim Lane, who was thought to be marching from the south in the rear of General Price. A cavalry detachment from Marshall's command went along with Peabody, carrying the funds from the Lexington bank. Accompanied by two officers of the Farmers' Bank, the cavalry detachment planned to take the funds to St. Louis for deposit there.[25]

At Warrensburg, Peabody also planned to rendezvous with Colonel James A. Mulligan, who was supposed to be camped there while on his way to Lexington with the Twenty-third Illinois Infantry, commonly called the "Irish Brigade" because of the large number of Irishmen in its ranks, even though it was just a regiment. Peabody reached Warrensburg on September 9 but did not form a junction with Mulligan, who had already departed for Lexington. Accompanied by about three hundred men of the Twenty-seventh Mounted Infantry Missouri Volunteers (formerly known as the Johnson County Home Guard), the Irish Brigade arrived at Lexington the same day Peabody reached Warrensburg. With orders from General Fremont to fortify the place and with the understanding that he would soon be reinforced, Mulligan took command of the Lexington post and began digging entrenchments, constructing earthworks, and enlarging the defenses already there. The supply of entrenching tools was inadequate; so a thorough search was made throughout the town, and, according to a *Chicago Tribune* report, "every description of suitable or available implements appropriated. The work was pushed with vigor, the heavy muscle of the brigade telling well as the brave fellows toiled in the trenches."[26]

Chapter 3

THE MARCH TO LEXINGTON

After marching south in late June, the separate Missouri State Guard forces under Governor Jackson and General Rains reunited near the end of the month at Lamar, where additional recruits were being mustered into service. Resuming the march south, the Missouri State Guard clashed at the Battle of Carthage on July 5, 1861, with about 1,100 Federal troops under Colonel Franz Sigel, whom General Lyon had sent to southwest Missouri from St. Louis after the Planters Hotel meeting. Although many of Jackson's approximately 5,500 men were unarmed or poorly armed, Sigel was at last forced to retreat before the superior numbers, leaving the field in the hands of the state troops. General Price, who was camped farther south, missed the Battle of Carthage, but he arrived the next day to join in celebrating the victory.[1]

After the Battle of Carthage, Price spent about three weeks in the southwest corner of Missouri training and equipping his Missouri State Guard. Then, in late July, he joined forces with General McCulloch's Confederate army and Arkansas state troops under General N. Bart Pearce and marched toward Springfield, where Lyon had rendezvoused on July 13 with Sigel and other Federal forces previously sent to southwest Missouri from St. Louis. On August 10, the two sides met at the Battle of Wilson's Creek, about ten miles southwest of Springfield, in the first important battle of the Civil War west of the Mississippi. Although casualties were about equal (slightly fewer than three hundred killed and about one thousand wounded on each side), General Lyon was killed in the action, and the Union forces

Colonel Franz Sigel's Union forces were defeated by Governor
Jackson's Missouri State Guard at the Battle of Carthage. *Courtesy of the
Library of Congress.*

retreated from the field. Thus, the Battle of Wilson's Creek was an important
victory for the Southern forces and a demoralizing defeat for the Union
effort in Missouri.

General Price hoped to follow up on the achievement by marching north
and breaking the Union's stronghold on the Missouri River, thus allowing
the Southern squads and companies that had been organizing on the
north side to join his army. He dared to dream of taking possession of the
whole state, which, if accomplished, would go a long way toward turning

Nathaniel Lyon, Union general, was killed at the Battle of
Wilson's Creek. *General Nathaniel Lyon, #31752, in the collection of
Wilson's Creek National Battlefield. Courtesy of the National Park Service.*

the tide of the war in favor of the South. He felt that Southern sympathies
were overwhelming throughout the state, that new recruits would flock to
his army, and that the people of northern Missouri would welcome him
and his men as liberators. General McCulloch, however, declined to go
along on the mission. He disliked Price in the first place and particularly
detested what he saw as a lack of discipline among the Missouri State
Guard troops. He told Price his army was needed to protect Arkansas
and Indian Territory and that many of his troops were getting ready to

Ben McCulloch, Confederate general, declined General Price's request to accompany the Missouri State Guard north from Springfield. *Ben McCulloch, #31500, in the collection of Wilson's Creek National Battlefield. Courtesy of the National Park Service.*

return home. In addition, he said that a movement into north Missouri could not be sustained without the support of Confederate forces in the eastern part of the state, and those forces had recently withdrawn to the Arkansas border.[2]

Angry but not deterred by McCulloch's stance, Price headed north out of Springfield on August 25, commanding an army of about seven thousand men. He had previously learned of raids into Missouri by U.S. senator Jim Lane's fledgling Kansas Brigade and had sent General Rains to clear out what he called the "murdering and marauding bands" infesting the border area. Informed that the Federals were gathering in force near Fort Scott and that Rains needed reinforcements, Price turned west at Bolivar and marched toward Kansas. On September 2, the Missouri State Guard skirmished with Lane's forces in western Vernon County at the Battle of Dry Wood Creek. Casualties were light on both sides, but General Lane's small army was forced to retire before Price's advancing hordes. Two days later, from his camp near Fort Scott, General Price reported to Governor Jackson that he had driven Lane from Missouri and that the Federals had also abandoned Fort Scott, thereby relieving Price of the need to pursue them into Kansas, which he did not want to do unless he learned of "renewed outrages" on the people of Missouri by Lane's army. Price added that "the desperate conflict at Springfield" had turned his men into veteran soldiers to whom skirmishes like the Battle of Dry Wood Creek were "but trifles."[3]

Kansas senator Jim Lane's forces were defeated by the Missouri State Guard at the Battle of Dry Wood Creek. *Courtesy of the Library of Congress.*

Some of the soldiers in Price's army questioned the decision not to invade Kansas. John Wyatt, an irascible and outspoken surgeon in General James H. McBride's Seventh Division of the Missouri State Guard, was particularly displeased. Upon learning that the troops had been ordered "to take the backtrack," Captain Wyatt told his diary, "Did not like this much as we wanted to give the Jayhawkers hell on their own territory—we only gave them a taste of what we would like to give them. Had we reached Fort Scott we would have done so too."[4]

Like most of his fellow soldiers, Wyatt initially had no idea where Price was headed, but by the time of the Dry Wood Creek fight, he had learned the army's destination. "So on we go to Lexington," he concluded his September 4 diary entry, "where I hope we may come up with the Dam Dutch and not let them get bye so easy as they did at Fort Scott."[5]

A variety of factors likely entered into Price's decision to target Lexington. It was strategically located on the Missouri River in the middle of the state, surrounded by Southern-sympathizing counties. In addition, it was probably considered an easier target than similarly situated Union posts like Boonville and Jefferson City. Also, Price and his men were already familiar with Lexington, having rendezvoused and briefly trained there in June. Intelligence gained, too, from men like Shelby who had laid siege to the town in late August might well have helped shape the final decision to march on Lexington.

After lingering a few days in the Nevada area because of heavy rains, Price resumed the march north on September 6, traveling fifteen to twenty miles a day. On the evening of September 8, he camped on the South Grand River near where the Bates and Cass County lines meet the Henry County line. Governor Jackson came into camp from the south and made a speech to the men, which, according to Captain Wyatt, "was received with wild enthusiasm."[6]

On September 9, the march continued almost due north, picking up new recruits along the way, as Price had anticipated. Near the small community of Index in Cass County, Colonel Routt, with several hundred men from the Missouri River counties of western Missouri, came down and joined the parade. In fact, according to Price, his numbers increased by the hour. "Like a moving ball of snow," as one soldier phrased it, "the further his army went the more it grew." Many of the would-be warriors, however, were poorly armed, as had been the case with the first recruits earlier in the year.[7]

Crossing into Johnson County from Index, Price went into camp on the afternoon of the ninth west of Rose Hill. He had just stopped for the day when he got word that a detachment of Federals (Peabody's command) was marching from Lexington to Warrensburg "to rob the bank in that place and plunder and arrest the citizens of Johnson County, in accordance with General Fremont's proclamation and instructions." Although his troops were weary, Price, or Old Pap as his men often called him, determined to press forward and try to surprise the Federals at Warrensburg. After allowing a couple of hours for the men to rest and the cavalry to feed their horses, he took up the march again about sundown and didn't stop

Colonel Everett Peabody retreated from Warrensburg in the face of Price's advance. *Everett Peabody, #30677, in the collection of Wilson's Creek National Battlefield. Courtesy of the National Park Service.*

until almost 2:00 a.m., when he finally called a halt because the exhausted infantry, many of whom had had little or nothing to eat, could go no farther. Price then pressed forward with the cavalry but learned, upon reaching the outskirts of Warrensburg about dawn on the morning of the tenth, that Peabody had abandoned the town about midnight. Price's infantry and artillery reached Warrensburg later that morning, but their fatigue and hunger, combined with heavy rains that had begun falling, convinced Price to postpone a pursuit.[8]

Peabody's retreat from Warrensburg was so rapid that, unable to see very well in the darkness, the Federals overturned and broke a couple of their wagons and were forced to burn them to keep the supplies from falling into the hands of the Rebels. They also burned the bridges over the Blackwater River and Davis Creek to retard the Southern pursuit. Meanwhile, Peabody sent a runner ahead to Lexington to inform Colonel Mulligan that Price was in close pursuit, and Mulligan began throwing up entrenchments at an even more urgent pace than before. He also dispatched messengers to various Union posts seeking reinforcements, including a squad of twelve men aboard the steamboat *Sunshine* bound for Jefferson City and an overland messenger bound for the same destination. The latter carried a dispatch that read, "Ten or fifteen thousand men, under Price, Jackson & Co., are reported near Warrensburg, moving on to this post. We will hold out. Strengthen us; we will require it."[9]

During the day of the tenth, the citizens of Warrensburg, said Price, "vied with each other in feeding my almost famished soldiers." The author of the 1881 *History of Lafayette County* also remembered that "the good people of Warrensburg" fed and cared for the Southern army to the best of their ability. Apparently, however, there was not enough food to go around. John J. Sitton, a color-bearer in the Seventh Division, recalled, "Rain fell all day on the 10th and we were all wet to the skin and could not cook anything." Another soldier complained that "every eatable of any consequence had been used up or destroyed by the Federal command" and it was "after midnight before supper was ready."[10]

Despite the late supper, the troops were back on the road to Lexington on the morning of September 11, the cavalry again taking the lead. Some of the horses began to break down during the hard gallop, but Price pushed forward, still hoping to overtake the Federals. Both his cavalry and the trailing infantry were greeted warmly by Southern-sympathizing citizens along the road. Private Sitton remembered that many of them came out "with buckets and pitchers of water and in some cases with cakes and coffee that they handed to our soldiers as we marched by."[11]

Peabody, still accompanied by Marshall's cavalry detachment, reached Lexington about dusk on the evening of the eleventh with word that Price was close on his heels. Mulligan took charge of the money confiscated from the Farmers' Bank and buried it under his tent. He also sent out a detachment under Captain Dan Quirk of the Irish Brigade with two pieces of artillery, supported by two companies of Peabody's regiment, to command a covered bridge a couple miles south of town on the present-

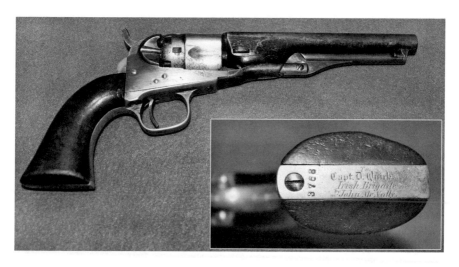

Revolver that belonged to Captain Dan Quirk of the Irish Brigade, with accompanying inscription. *Courtesy of Joe Maghe.*

day Higginsville Road that Price would have to cross on his approach to Lexington.[12]

Meanwhile, Price was met by persons coming out from Lexington to tell him that the Federals were already back in town, and he called a halt to the march and went into camp about two and a half miles from Lexington. Among his cavalry was Ephraim Anderson, the young man who had been unable to cross the Missouri River after the Boonville skirmish in June, but he had finally joined Price near Fort Scott. Remembering the September 11 camp outside Lexington, he said, "We…halted in a woodland pasture and bivouacked for the night, eating roasted corn for supper."[13]

Chapter 4

LEXINGTON

September 12, 1861

According to Colonel Mulligan, the night of September 11 was "a night of fearful anxiety," but "the hours passed in silence." Apparently, however, not complete silence. Both Price, guarding his camp, and the Union detachment, guarding the approach to Lexington, threw out pickets, and there was some minor skirmishing between the opposing sentries during the night. Isaac Hockaday, a citizen who lived on the outskirts of Lexington near the covered bridge, wrote to his mother two days later that Peabody had scarcely gotten back to town on the evening of the eleventh when "the advance picket guard of Jackson's men…drove in the Federal pickets. They unhorsed one of them & ripped and tore through our yard & Barn lot on the hunt of him." From that time until early the following morning, Hockaday added, there was continual firing between the pickets of both sides along the road that ran in front of his house, and a Union soldier described the skirmishing on the night of the eleventh as "heavy but indecisive." Most sources, however, make no mention of fighting on the night of the eleventh, and any skirmishing that occurred was probably minimal.[1]

On the morning of September 12, though, a sharp skirmish between the Union outposts and the Southern pickets broke out when Price's cavalry began crossing the covered bridge shortly after dawn. Watching through a looking glass from atop College Hill, Mulligan could see Price's movements, and he ordered out two more companies of Peabody's infantry and another company from the Irish Brigade to support the detachment that had kept the night vigil. Isaac Hockaday had gone over to a neighbor's house about

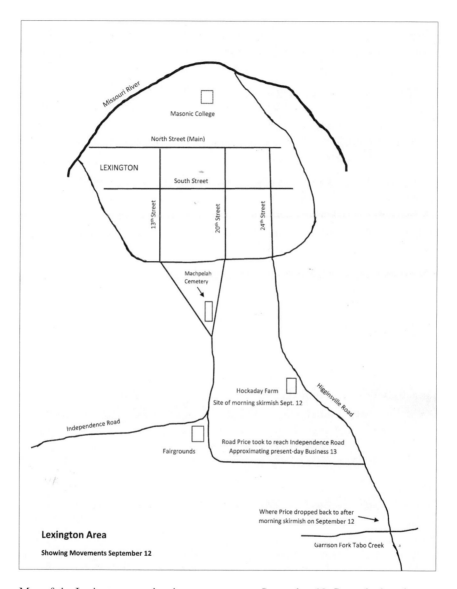

Map of the Lexington area showing movements on September 12. *Drawn by the author.*

daylight to suggest moving the two families out of harm's way when the skirmish broke out, cutting him off from his home and family. Hockaday finally got one of the Union soldiers to escort him home, but in the meantime, the two sides "got into a hot skirmish in my corn & hemp fields which lasted until ten o'clock in the day."[2]

Price's advance formed in a line across and to the west of the road along a fence that enclosed Hockaday's field. The Federal skirmishers, composed of Company H of Peabody's command and Company B of Van Horn's battalion, faced the Southerners from atop a hill about three hundred yards away. The Federals, "covering themselves behind the hemp-shocks," according to Ephraim Anderson, "opened fire with their long-range guns; they were only visible when stepping out to fire, but the glitter of bayonets was very distinct all the while behind every hemp-shock. Our guns could not reach them, and it was not the inclination of the commander-in-chief to waste ammunition in unnecessary skirmishing."[3]

Unwilling to risk a general engagement with a dubious outcome, Price decided to drop back, and he had already withdrawn before the additional companies Mulligan sent out reached the scene of the skirmish. Price retreated two or three miles back toward Warrensburg before stopping near Garrison Creek to wait for his infantry and artillery. After his withdrawal, the Federals burned the covered bridge that they had guarded during the night.[4]

When Price's infantry and artillery came up in the early afternoon, the Missouri State Guard resumed its march toward Lexington. About three miles south of town, Price detoured through a lane toward the Independence Road so as to approach the town from a more westerly direction. About 2:00 p.m., near where the lane intersected the Independence Road, Price's advance met a party of Federal cavalry acting as pickets and drove them into town. Gaining the Independence Road, the state troops continued their march to Lexington.[5]

Warned of Price's approach, Colonel Mulligan sent out four companies from Peabody's Thirteenth Missouri and two companies from Van Horn's battalion, and they concealed themselves in some hedges and cornfields to the east of the road about a mile south of town near Machpelah Cemetery. When the Southerners neared the cemetery about 3:00 p.m., the Federals opened fire from a distance of about 150 yards on a regiment of cavalry that formed the State Guard advance. The cavalrymen returned fire, but their horses quickly became unmanageable, forcing them to retreat and dismount.[6]

In a letter to his wife a couple days later, John A. Thomas, who was among the Missouri State Guard infantry just to the rear of the cavalry (but on the opposite side of the road), described the confusion among the Southern ranks caused by the initial Federal volley: "The first thing we knew we were right on the enemy. They commenced firing at our men out of a corn field across a lane from us. There was a lot of our cavalry between our regiment and [the] enemy, which run over several of our company scattering them so some of them never got with their company any more the whole evening."[7]

Led by a regiment of General Parsons's division under Captain Rock Champion, the Missouri State Guard infantry advanced and opened a galling fire, but the Federals stood their ground at first. The two sides exchanged several volleys before Bledsoe's and Captain Henry Guibor's batteries came up and fired a few artillery rounds to help dislodge the bluecoats from their position. In addition, as more and more of Price's army hurried to the front, the Missouri State

Colonel Robert Van Horn's forces participated in the skirmishing at Machpelah Cemetery. *Missouri Valley Special Collections, Kansas City Public Library, Kansas City, Missouri.*

Guard's vastly superior numbers threatened to flank the Federals and cut them off from the fort. According to Thomas, the Federals retreated "in the greatest confusion, we following like so many wolves yelling with all their might after their prey."[8]

As the Union soldiers withdrew toward town, a portion of General McBride's command crossed the road and passed through an orchard into the cemetery to give pursuit. Emerging from the cemetery, the Southern troops entered a street but quickly came to a low, open area where McBride paused to re-form his line. When Colonel Edmund T. Wingo, commander of a cavalry regiment, and Al Edgar Asbury, McBride's aide-de-camp, rode forward to the top of a rise to reconnoiter, Wingo was shot from the saddle by Union fire from a concealed position behind some buildings ahead. Dismounting, Asbury managed to get Wingo back on his horse, and the two retreated safely to McBride's main line. When McBride's men came up and returned fire, the Federals once again, according to the general, "fled like rats and did not halt until safely landed within their entrenchments."[9]

The skirmishing near the cemetery lasted, according to one Missouri State Guard officer, about thirty minutes. (Although Mulligan described this

Machpelah Cemetery as it appears today. *Courtesy of Patrick Keller.*

skirmish near the cemetery as one in which "the fight raged furiously over the dead," very little, if any, of the fighting actually occurred in the graveyard.) Southern losses totaled at least two killed, one mortally wounded, several seriously wounded, and several others with minor wounds. Meanwhile, the Union had at least one man mortally wounded, two severely, and four slightly. In addition, two companies of the Irish Brigade mistakenly opened fire on Peabody and Van Horn's men as they were retreating to the entrenchments, wounding one of them before the goof was discovered.[10]

One of the badly wounded Rebels was Colonel Wingo, who was shot through the shoulder. He later recovered sufficiently to resume his service in the Missouri State Guard, but he recalled years after the war, "The ball that tore my shoulder to pieces knocked all the love of military glory out of me."[11]

The State Guard chased the fleeing Federals into town, driving most of them into their fortifications. Some of Price's cavalry and infantry got within close enough range of the college fort to exchange shots with some of the Federals ensconced behind their earthworks and entrenchments. At one point, a State Guard soldier even managed to plant a Southern flag inside the line of entrenchments. However, Price's cavalry and infantry were quickly driven back, and this skirmishing resulted in few, if any, casualties.[12]

Once Price's horsemen and foot soldiers dropped back, the clash on the late afternoon of the twelfth became almost exclusively an artillery duel. Bledsoe's battery, which was part of General Rains's Eighth Division, took up a position southeast of the Federal entrenchments near where the Wentworth Academy is now located, and Henry Guibor's battery of General Parsons's division unlimbered in the same general vicinity, both within "easy range of the college," according to General Price. Parsons placed the distance more specifically at about six hundred yards.[13]

Bledsoe's battery, commanded by Captain Emmett MacDonald in the absence of Hiram Bledsoe, who had been wounded at Dry Wood Creek, opened "a brisk fire" upon the Union fortifications, according to Price, and Parsons's battery, "under the skillful command of Captain Guibor," joined in the cannonade. The Southerners also fired a volley of grapeshot toward a group of mounted Federal officers who happened to be outside the breastworks, producing what Colonel Mulligan called "an amusing effect" among the officers. They came charging into the breastworks but claimed they did so only because of the panic of their horses. At the same time, some of the soldiers inside the breastworks went scampering to the safer confines of the surrounding trenches.[14]

One Union officer who did not move with alacrity when the State Guard barrage began was the Irish Brigade's three-hundred-pound quartermaster, Quin Morton. A Federal soldier later recalled that Morton, "indifferent to danger," was "perched on a stump in direct range of all the bullets and presenting as

Emmett MacDonald commanded Bledsoe's battery in Hiram Bledsoe's absence during the early part of the siege. *Emmett MacDonald, #30826, in the collection of Wilson's Creek National Battlefield. Courtesy of the National Park Service.*

fine a target to the enemy as the horses that were being killed and crippled around him."[15]

When the big guns of the State Guard first opened on the Federal entrenchments, the scene inside the breastworks was, according to Mulligan, one of "the wildest confusion. Each man evidently believed that he who made the most noise was doing the most shooting. Those who were not shooting at the moon were shooting above it, into the earth, or elsewhere at random, in the wildest, most reckless manner." To conserve ammunition and try to restore a sense of discipline among the ranks, Mulligan ordered his men to cease firing while he gave them impromptu instructions on how to fire with more precision. Soon, Mulligan said, everything was moving "as cleverly as a Yankee clock."[16]

Calling into service three pieces of artillery that were planted in front of the college, the Federals replied vigorously to the State Guard barrage, and the firing became "quick and incessant on both sides," as Southern cavalryman Ephraim Anderson described the cannonading. A Union soldier inside the breastwork had a similar but no doubt closer-up perspective on the bombardment. "It is not very pleasant to have cannon balls flying all around and over me," Lieutenant Thomas D. McClure told his diary just an hour or so after the shelling ended. "One poor fellow had his head taken off with a ball, another one both legs. A ball passed over us, went through three mules which stood in range, and they did not impede the momentum of the ball apparently in the least, but it went tearing, crashing along, like some infuriated thing."[17]

At one point during the heaviest part of the fighting, according to Private Anderson, General Price, heedless of the danger, galloped to the front to personally direct the artillery. "Perfectly self-possessed, he seemed not to heed the storm of grape and canister…Many of the officers urged him to retire or dismount, but with perfect coolness he kept his position." Even after a grapeshot struck his field glasses, breaking them to pieces, he showed not "the slightest apparent emotion." When he finally retired after about twenty minutes, his bravery had left a lasting impression on his men, who ever after, according to Anderson, "loved him as their chief and admired him as their 'beau ideal' of honor and chivalry."[18]

Not all of Price's men, however, shared Anderson's high opinion of their leader. Writing home just a few days after the action Anderson described, William S. Hyde, a colonel in the Third Division, admitted that Price was a brave man who exposed himself in battle, but he felt Price was "lacking in generalship." Hyde added, "We have never had any discipline—have

Sterling Price, commanding general of the Missouri State Guard. *Courtesy of the Library of Congress.*

scarcely the organization of an effective mob."[19]

Lieutenant William P. Barlow, an officer in Guibor's battery, related an amusing incident that occurred toward the end of the artillery exchange. A Federal six-pound shot went tearing through one of the battery's powder caissons, shredding and igniting a bundle of port fires and scattering them around as they began fizzing and sputtering. Captain Rock Champion, who happened to be nearby, "stood in their midst," according to Barlow, "and, too proud to run in the presence of his men, drew himself up waiting to be blown to pieces, calling out: 'Hello, Guibor, what the d_____ kind of an infernal machine is this they're throwing at you?' Guibor simply laughed in reply, and Rock, much relieved, relaxed his rigid attitude and tried to laugh too, but it was a weak attempt."[20]

The State Guard was already short on ammunition because most of its ordnance wagons had been left at Osceola, far to the south, and the shredded caisson didn't help. As darkness began to set in, Price's ammunition was running low, his men were tired and hungry, and two and a half hours of bombarding the Federal position had produced little advantage. Old Pap decided to withdraw and wait for his supply train to come up.[21]

Overall casualties on September 12 were relatively small on both sides. A correspondent to the *Chicago Post* who was in the fight on the Union side placed the Federal loss, including the skirmishing earlier in the afternoon, at eight killed and fifteen wounded. Although casualties on the side of the state troops is less certain, one estimate placed the total loss in killed and wounded at about twenty-five. This again includes casualties from both the early afternoon skirmish near the cemetery and the cannonading later in the day. Perhaps Private Thomas summed it up best in a letter to his wife shortly after the action. Claiming the Southerners lost only one or two killed and just a few wounded, he continued, "I know nothing of the loss of the enemy, but if it was no more than ours, I don't see why, for our men faught [*sic*] like perfect demons."[22]

After Price's withdrawal, Mulligan called his officers together and asked their opinions on what course of action to pursue next. Nearly all the subordinate officers advised that the best thing to do was to evacuate the fortifications. Lieutenant Colonel White suggested crossing the Missouri River on two steamboats docked at the nearby landing northwest of the college fort, while Colonel Peabody, volunteering his regiment to lead the way, argued for marching toward Sedalia, even if they had to fight their way through. But the ambitious Mulligan, an Irish Catholic attorney back in Chicago and a rising military officer, had a different idea. At the end of the meeting, after letting his officers voice their views, the thirty-one-year-old colonel overruled them. "Gentlemen," he said, "I have heard what you have to say, but, begad, we'll fight 'em! That's what we enlisted for, and that's what we'll do."[23]

Price encamped that night at the fairgrounds south of Lexington and dubbed the place Camp Wallace after local judge and Southern-sympathizer Henry Wallace. With Governor Jackson in attendance, Price, like his Union counterpart, also held a council of war. A couple of officers wanted to resume the assault as soon as possible, but most of them, including General Price, decided against useless bloodshed. Knowing his ammunition wagon was en route and that additional men would soon be arriving to augment his already considerable advantage in numbers, Price felt that a Federal surrender was just a matter of time. "We've got 'em, dead sure," he reportedly told his officers. "All we have to do is watch 'em."[24]

Meanwhile, the Missouri troops prepared supper and "ate with appetites sharpened by long fasting," according to Ephraim Anderson. "A couch of down could not have made my sleep more sound and refreshing than it was that night."[25]

Chapter 5

LEXINGTON

September 13–16, 1861

O n the late night of September 12 and during the wee hours of September 13, with the Southern troops lying south of town on and near the fairgrounds, Mulligan continued the work of strengthening his fortifications. About dawn on the morning of the thirteenth, Lieutenant McClure recorded that he had been up all night standing sentry for the men working on the embankments.[1]

Later the same morning, General Parsons sent in a flag of truce asking that the Southerners be allowed to carry away and bury their dead, and he reminded Mulligan that he had granted the same courtesy to Federals at Wilson's Creek after General Lyon had fallen. Mulligan granted the request but felt insulted that Parsons deemed it necessary "to quote any precedent to the Irish Brigade for an act of humanity."[2]

Writing a number of years after the war, Richard H. Musser, who was a lieutenant colonel and judge advocate general in Colonel Congreve Jackson's Third Division at Lexington, said that he, as flag bearer, led the detail that was sent in on the mission to retrieve the dead. Colonel George K. Dills of Parsons's division was one of those reportedly killed in the previous day's skirmishing, and Musser was especially concerned about Dills, since the two had known each other as boys growing up in Kentucky. Musser recalled that the detail was met by Frederick Becker, whose rank as a major Mulligan had reinstated "by courtesy." Becker recognized Musser as a passenger who had traveled with him between Brunswick and Carrollton prior to the war when Becker was a stage driver. Musser was briefly detained in a house, but he was soon assured that Colonel Dills was not dead and that he was being treated for a buckshot wound at the nearby home of Silas Silver (the man accused earlier in the year of being a secret secessionist). Taken to the Silver residence, Musser found Dills "more in danger of dying of love for his fair nurse than from his wounds."[3]

According to Lieutenant McClure, a second detail from Price's army came in under a separate flag of truce on the same day requesting an exchange of prisoners. Little else is known, however, about the result of this second mission.[4]

A drenching rain began on the morning of the thirteenth, but in the words of Colonel Mulligan, "the work of throwing up the entrenchments went on, and the men stood almost knee deep in mud and water at their work." At three o'clock in the afternoon, Lieutenant McClure recorded that he and his comrades had "stood in this ditch all the time and are cold, wet, and weary."[5]

The Federal fortifications, when completed, consisted of a rectangular earthworks enclosing the Masonic College and an irregular line of outer entrenchments along the brow of College Hill encircling the main fort. Northwest of the college toward the river but within the outer line of entrenchments was another brick building that had previously been used as the college dormitory. The main earthworks around the college had bastions at the corners with barbettes and embrasures for the firing of cannons, and the walls were about eight to ten feet high and twelve feet thick, making them impenetrable to cannon fire. A ditch about six feet deep and twelve feet wide outside the wall served to further obstruct an enemy attack. The outer entrenchments consisted of a series of smaller embankments with a dugout area on the inside and a larger ditch outside containing a traverse of sharp spikes and other obstructions. Beyond the ditch were what Mulligan called "confusion pits," and the Federals also set mines between the pits that could be discharged at the approach of the enemy. The mines consisted of buried powder with fuses threaded through metal pipes that had been ripped from the Masonic College. The line of outer entrenchments was about two hundred feet from the main fort except to the west and northwest, where it swept away eight hundred feet down the hill toward the river. Encompassing about fifteen acres, the fortifications were made large enough to accommodate about ten thousand men, since Mulligan was expecting reinforcements.[6]

Outside the line of entrenchments to the west sat a two-and-a-half-story brick building. Previously the private residence of wealthy hemp manufacturer Oliver Anderson, the Federals turned it into a hospital, and a few rifle pits

What remains today of the line of entrenchments on the northwest promontory of College Hill. *Photo by the author.*

between the hospital and the line of entrenchments reinforced this location. The land beyond the Anderson home to the northwest dropped off at a steep declivity toward the river a half mile away, and the hillside was covered with scattered timber, while the area directly north of the fortifications was also hilly and wooded. The area south and southeast of the fortifications, on the other hand, consisted of relatively level, open fields. Since this was the only direction from which an infantry or cavalry attack was considered feasible, the outer entrenchments were strongest here. At least two sally ports, one located on the south side of the fortifications and another near the Anderson house, allowed for the entry and exit of Union troops. Several springs from which the Federals fetched water were located outside the lines, including one north of the Masonic College on the east side of the fortifications, one in a ravine west-southwest of the college, and another one farther west near the Anderson house. Inside the lines, near the college, were also two or three cisterns to supply water for the needs of the troops. Mulligan declined a suggestion by one of his engineers to have additional cisterns or wells dug. He felt that the Federal horses and mules, which were corralled in a designated area inside the fortifications, could be watered at the Missouri River, since the Federal position commanded access to the river.[7]

The Anderson house as it appears today. *Photo by the author.*

Mulligan's total strength was about 2,800 men. This included about 900 soldiers of the Irish Brigade, about 800 in Peabody and Van Horn's combined command, about 500 Illinois cavalrymen under Colonel Marshall, and about 600 home guards from Lafayette and Johnson Counties. Most contemporaneous estimates placed the total Union strength at 3,500, while a few had it as low as 2,000. However, Mulligan himself said he had "a little garrison of 2,700," and at another point he placed the exact number at 2,780, which was probably quite accurate.[8]

In the basement of the Masonic College, Mulligan set up a makeshift foundry, and some of the Illinois cavalry under Captain John McNulta had previously taken charge of Morrison's foundry, located northwest of the fortifications near the river. Altogether, Mulligan had 150 rounds of grapeshot and canister cast for each of his five six-pound cannons. The Union forces also had two mortars for throwing spherical shells but had only 40 shells available.[9]

Mulligan procured a quantity of powder as well, and the men began making cartridges for their individual weapons. Most of the Federals, with the exception of the First Illinois Cavalry, were fairly well armed. Marshall's cavalry, however, had only swords and "one barreled horse pistols," as Private George H. Palmer, a bugler in the regiment, called the old-style dragoons the men had been issued at St. Louis. "The swords were rotten and the

John McNulta of the First Illinois Cavalry cast shot for the Union at Morrison's foundry during the days leading up to the Battle of Lexington. *Courtesy of the McClean County Museum of History.*

pistols were worthless," Palmer complained.[10]

Meanwhile on the thirteenth, the Missouri State Guard troops spent a wet day at their camp headquartered on the fairgrounds. Captain Wyatt recorded in his diary that it was "raining like Hell...Rain, Rain, Rain." Despite the miserable weather, though, reinforcements continued to stream in. About 1,100 men arrived on the thirteenth from Independence. (These men were likely under Colonel Reid.) As Ephraim Anderson recalled, "Detachments were dropping in every day, sometimes small, then in larger force."[11]

After Price established his headquarters at the fairgrounds on the night of the twelfth, the Southern soldiers set up their camps on or near the fairgrounds, many in the direction of town, and they threw out pickets about a half mile from the town. The Federals also established lookouts surrounding their fortifications, about four hundred yards from the State Guard sentinels, and beginning on the thirteenth, skirmishing broke out sporadically between the two sides. As Susan McCausland remembered, "During these days of waiting continual skirmishing went on between the soldiers in town and small squads of those outside." Ephraim Anderson recalled that the skirmishing was usually occasioned by taunts and dares hurled between the opposing pickets: "Occasionally, they called to us to come down; we would respond that they had better come to us. Sometimes they would gallop up within a hundred and fifty yards and fire, and then promptly run back." Having no orders to drive the Federal pickets in, the Southerners would allow the Union sentries to reclaim the protection of their haystacks or other shelter. According to a Federal lieutenant, from the night of the twelfth until the main battle began on the eighteenth, the state troops "kept up a constant fire of musketry from the house tops and windows of the town upon the entrenchments."[12]

During a skirmish on the morning of the thirteenth, some Rebel sharpshooters took shelter in some cornfields and houses not far from the Union fortifications to hide themselves from view of the Union pickets. Thirty-nine-year-old Colonel Reid took part in this skirmish or a similar one near the same time and reportedly distinguished himself for gallantry and recklessness in exposing himself to the enemy. After the fighting died down and the Southerners retired, Colonel Mulligan sent out a detail to cut down the offending corn and to burn the houses.[13]

One Federal picket, George Palmer, dared to venture out beyond the Union lines. On the thirteenth, he rode out on a scouting mission to an area of town between the opposing outposts and found, holed up in a private residence, a Southern surgeon attending a slightly wounded artilleryman. Palmer took the two men prisoner and brought them back to the Union fortifications, where Mulligan paroled the surgeon but kept the artilleryman as a prisoner.[14]

Susan McCausland and other Southern-sympathizing citizens of Lexington sometimes went out to visit Price's camp during the lull in fighting that began on the night of the twelfth. "The thin line of Federal pickets," she said, "was no stay to the adventurous who might wish to go out." It was very likely people such as Mrs. McCausland that Captain Wyatt had in mind when he complained shortly after the Southerners set up camp at the fairgrounds, "Confound this town fighting, the women and children running and screaming all over town. They rushed into our camp from everywhere more afraid of the Dutch than they are of our guns."[15]

The Federals were baffled on the morning of September 13 and again on the fourteenth when Price did not renew his attack of the twelfth. Lieutenant McClure surmised that the Southerners were either trying to induce the Federals to come outside their fortifications, waiting for more arms and more men, or else retreating. Reasoning that all these possible motives for a delay in the State Guard attack were ridiculous, McClure brashly concluded that the Southerners must be afraid. He was reinforced in his bold opinion by a State Guard officer taken prisoner during the skirmishing on the twelfth (probably Colonel Dills) who stated to his Union captors that Price had expected to find only the home guard on duty at the Lexington post.[16]

Still, despite Price's stalling tactics, McClure knew that a renewed attack was just a matter of time. "No doubt," he told his diary on the morning of the fourteenth, "we will have a bloody, fearful contest yet."[17]

General John C. Fremont's feeble efforts to reinforce Lexington failed. *Courtesy of the Library of Congress.*

The same day, McClure complained to his diary that additional Union reinforcements had not reached Lexington. "It is a great pity," he said, "that Gen. Fremont has not sent forward more men. If we are finally beaten it will rest upon him, not us."[18]

Fremont, who had also been roundly criticized for his failure to reinforce General Lyon at Wilson's Creek, was, in fact, making halfhearted efforts to strengthen Lexington. However, the Southern forces were busy doing whatever they could to impede those efforts. The *Sunshine*, which Mulligan dispatched to Jefferson City on the tenth seeking reinforcements, was captured late the next day at Glasgow by Rebel forces under Colonel Martin Green of General Thomas Harris's division, which was on its way from north Missouri to reinforce Price. Rendezvousing with Green, Harris used the confiscated boat to ferry his troops across the river on the twelfth. The bulk of his men then started overland toward Lexington, taking the crew of the *Sunshine* along as prisoners, while a detachment of his command started back up the river aboard the *Sunshine*. Stopping for the night, the boat and its new crew were lying in dock at Cambridge when Federal soldiers shot the steamer full of holes, but the Rebels made their escape and started marching overland toward Lexington to join their comrades.[19]

Fremont was hesitant to move large numbers of troops away from St. Louis and eastern Missouri to reinforce Lexington just as he had been loath to send troops to the western part of the state prior to Wilson's Creek, and in some cases, the sluggishness of his subordinate officers in carrying out his tentative orders only made matters worse. On September 12, when Colonel Jefferson C. Davis, commanding at Jefferson City, received the message that

Mulligan had dispatched by land on the tenth requesting reinforcements, Davis immediately wired Fremont with the urgent news of Price's advance on Lexington. Fremont responded on the thirteenth, ordering Davis to send two regiments to Lexington "provided nothing has occurred since your last dispatch to render it inexpedient." Fremont promised to send two regiments from St. Louis to Jefferson City to take the place of the ones sent to Lexington.[20]

But something, in fact, had occurred to render sending further reinforcements inexpedient, at least in Davis's mind. Prior to his communication with General Fremont, Davis had already sent supplies and a detachment of troops up the river aboard the steamboat *Sioux City* to reinforce Lexington, but upon encountering Harris's force near Glasgow, they had turned around and started back because, according to a contemporaneous newspaper report, they "found it impossible to run the fire which the rebels poured into them from the shore." Responding to Fremont's telegram, Davis proposed that he would try to prevent Harris from crossing the Missouri River, and he made no mention of whether he had sent the two regiments to Lexington that Fremont had ordered him to send. Then, upon learning that Harris had already crossed the river, Davis replied to Fremont a second time proposing to intercept Harris and prevent him from reaching Lexington, and he suggested that Brigadier General Samuel D. Sturgis, who was then operating along the Hannibal–St. Joseph Railroad in northern Missouri, be sent to the relief of Lexington. Under pressure from provisional Missouri governor Hamilton R. Gamble to reinforce Lexington, Fremont responded to Davis on the fourteenth reiterating his order that Davis should immediately send two regiments to Lexington and that Sturgis would repair to Jefferson City and assume command there. Apparently, it was not until after receiving this order that Davis informed Fremont of his prior ill-fated attempt to reinforce Lexington because later the same day Fremont countermanded the order, sending Sturgis to the relief of Lexington and allowing Davis to retain command at Jefferson City.[21]

The skies cleared on September 14, and the Federals' work in the trenches went on just as it had during the downpour of the day before. Both officers and enlisted men worked on the fortifications, and the work, according to a captain in Colonel Peabody's command, "was continued almost constantly night and day."[22]

While the trench work went on, the skirmishing between opposing pickets also continued. On the fourteenth or early on the fifteenth, during one of their forays into town, the Federals burned some more buildings that the State

Guard had used as shelter, and one of the buildings, which had apparently been used to store a quantity of powder, exploded with a huge bang.[23]

As the Federals toiled in the trenches, the officers of the Missouri State Guard, turning their attention to mundane matters as well, commenced drilling their men at the fairgrounds. "Most of our officers were comparatively unpracticed," Ephraim Anderson recalled, "but we began with alacrity, and made some progress."[24]

Some of the Southern men not on picket duty or involved in the drills had other work to do. Lieutenant Barlow remembered that Guibor's men took possession of a foundry in town and spent most of the lull that followed the September 12 skirmish casting solid shot and grape for the battery's guns.[25]

On Sunday, September 15, Father Thaddeus J. Butler, chaplain of the Irish Brigade, celebrated Mass on the hillside of the Masonic College grounds, and according to Colonel Mulligan, "All were considerably strengthened and encouraged by his words." After the church services, the Union soldiers mostly went back to their pick-and-shovel work, while a few of the more flagrant Sabbath breakers among them turned to "stealing provisions from the inhabitants round about."[26]

The same day, Private Palmer again ventured out beyond the Union lines, this time disguised as a civilian to infiltrate the enemy lines. Dressed in a checkered shirt, blue overalls, and an old straw hat, he "took French leave" and headed on foot southwest along the river toward the Southern camps. Stopped by a party of four mounted Rebels, he was grilled for several minutes before his story that he had just come from Kentucky and was staying with a widow woman in town and his "idiotic questions" seemed to disarm them somewhat. He asked if he could go into their camp with them, but they told him they weren't headed to camp and rode away. Continuing on his way, Palmer came to a house where another party of Rebels were temporarily encamped. When the owner of the house began to question him and said he didn't know the widow woman Palmer was supposedly staying with, Palmer told him that the woman had lived in Lexington only about six months. He then asked for a drink of water, swallowed it, and said it was getting late and he must be going. He started off in the direction he had been walking but, as soon as he was out of sight, quickly retraced his steps back to the fortifications. He reported what he had done to Colonel Mulligan, who, according to Palmer, complimented him on his bravery "when he ought to have given me a dressing down for leaving the camp."[27]

Informed by pickets on the evening of September 15 that Price had received a large number of reinforcements under General Harris, Lieutenant

McClure felt sure that the Southerners would launch an assault the next day. "It certainly looks like death," he recorded glumly, "but mark me now, this will be as hard a battle as will occur during the war."[28]

According to other sources, General Harris did not arrive until the following day, and it's not clear whether these sources were mistaken or the rumor McClure heard on the night of September 15 was premature. At any rate, Harris marched into Price's camp on either the fifteenth or sixteenth with about three thousand men and two pieces of artillery. His exhausted men were allowed to rest after their forced march from Glasgow.[29]

The arrival of Harris's division bolstered the Missouri State Guard's already lopsided advantage in numbers over the Federals stationed at the Masonic College, and that advantage would continue to swell over the next few days. Contemporaneous estimates of Price's total force at Lexington varied widely, with Federal sources largely overestimating his numbers and State Guard sources tending to minimize those numbers. Mulligan gauged the force facing him at about twenty-eight thousand, and Union newspaper estimates were even more extravagant. One of the more outlandish reports placed the number of Southern troops at Lexington at thirty-seven thousand actually engaged in the action and another ten thousand who were supposedly out of camp on marauding expeditions. On the other hand, some of the Southerners, while admitting to having huge numbers of men lolling about their camp, claimed to have only four or five thousand soldiers actively engaged.[30]

In his report of the action at Lexington, General Price did not give an estimate of his total strength, but writing after the war, a Missouri State Guard veteran, Captain Joseph A. Wilson, gave what seems to be a fairly credible estimate of the number of Southern troops actively engaged, placing the figure at ten to twelve thousand. Wilson's explanation of the inflated Union counts also seems reasonable. He said that a large number of unarmed recruits lying in camp and a large number of private citizens who came into town on the day of the Federal surrender got mixed in with the actual soldiers, many of whom had no uniforms, and got included in the estimates. Wilson's reckoning is probably fairly accurate, although, as Major Van Horn observed after the war, even many of the private citizens "had something to shoot with." So the number of men, including poorly armed recruits and private citizens, who took some small part in the action on the side of the state might have been as high as fifteen to twenty thousand, but nowhere near thirty-seven thousand or even the twenty-eight thousand surmised by Mulligan. The 1881 county history placed the total number at twenty-three thousand, but even that estimate seems slightly skewed toward the high side.[31]

Estimates of the number of artillery pieces available to the Missouri State Guard were not nearly as divergent as the estimates of their total force. Mulligan thought Price had thirteen pieces of cannon, while the most extravagant Union report placed the figure at twenty. The best estimate of the actual number was sixteen, about halfway between the Union's most conservative and most liberal estimates.[32]

On the evening of September 15, the Missouri State Guard sent a messenger into the Union camp under a white flag proposing that if the Federals would evacuate the place voluntarily, they would be allowed to leave with "the honors of war." According to Lieutenant McClure, Price also proposed that if the Union soldiers would lay down their arms and not fight anymore in Missouri, the state troops would do the same. Mulligan rejected both proposals out of hand. According to McClure, the colonel sent a reply back to Price saying, "*The Irish Brigade makes no compromise and never surrenders*, but if you give us a few more days we will drive you out of the State." If such an exchange, in fact, took place, Price's offer was likely but a ploy, and Mulligan's reply proved to be mere braggadocio.[33]

At the State Guard camp, reinforcements continued to come in. "Troops coming in all the time," Captain Wyatt noted on the sixteenth. "Another brass band from the Platte today."[34]

Price's show of force on the Missouri River aroused the Southern-sympathizing people throughout the region. Colonel Davis at Jefferson City, reporting to General Fremont, warned, "Secession feeling increasing and people rising."[35]

The soldiers camped at the fairgrounds, however, were starting to get restless. Colonel Hyde complained in a letter to his sister on the sixteenth that the troops had been lolling about the fairgrounds ever since their arrival last week and "everyone is asking why we do not go through with the battle…We are all in suspense and the men are grumbling on account of the delay."[36]

The cantankerous Captain Wyatt complained louder than anybody else. "Still in camp and on hand for a Battle when the boss says the word," he recorded. "Hell is full of better Generals." Wyatt fretted that poor leadership would spoil everything that had thus far been gained for the Southern cause in Missouri, but he consoled himself that the state forces had prevailed at Carthage, Wilson's Creek, and Dry Wood without a commander, and maybe they could do it again. "Maybe God will still be with us."[37]

Skirmishing between pickets intensified on the sixteenth, reflecting the growing impatience of the state troops during the lull in action. "Heavy picket fighting by day and by night," James J. Tucker, a captain in Rains's division, recorded in his company book.[38]

Meanwhile, General Fremont and his subordinates continued their desultory efforts to relieve Colonel Mulligan. Assured by Colonel Davis on September 15 and again on the sixteenth that Price was either at or marching on Lexington with about 14,000 men, Fremont ordered Brigadier General John Pope, commanding Union forces in north Missouri, to send additional troops to Lexington to bolster the reinforcements under Sturgis, who had already been ordered to that place. Pope had previously dispatched Colonel Robert F. Smith from St. Joseph and Lieutenant Colonel John Scott from Cameron to march south, form a junction at Liberty, and try to intercept a large body of Southern troops who had departed St. Joseph on the twelfth headed to Lexington. Scott left Cameron on the fifteenth with about 500 men of the Third Iowa Infantry, a squad of German artillerists to work one gun, and a handful of home guards, while Smith left St. Joseph about the same time with the Sixteen Illinois Infantry, two companies of the Thirty-ninth Ohio, 150 cavalrymen, and three pieces of artillery. After receiving Fremont's latest orders, Pope sent a second message to St. Joseph instructing Smith to continue to Lexington after taking care of his first assignment, but Smith had already left St. Joseph by the time the communication arrived. Meanwhile, Sturgis left Macon on a westbound train the night of September 16 with the Twenty-seventh Ohio Infantry and a portion of the Thirty-ninth Ohio. Arriving at Utica early the next morning, Sturgis disembarked and started marching south toward Lexington forty miles away. Also on the sixteenth, General Fremont ordered Colonel Davis to march from Jefferson City to Georgetown in Pettis County, break up a nest of 3,000 to 4,000 Rebels supposed to be roosting there, and then to continue toward Lexington to help relieve Mulligan. Davis, however, again proved dilatory in carrying out the order, replying to Fremont that he needed more men and supplies before undertaking such a mission.[39]

Chapter 6

SEPTEMBER 17 AND THE BATTLE OF BLUE MILLS LANDING

The Missouri State Guard troops from northwest Missouri who had left St. Joseph on September 12 bound for Lexington consisted of a regiment of infantry under Colonel Thomas Jefferson "Jeff" Patton from the Fourth Division, a battalion of cavalry under Lieutenant Colonel Richard "Dick" Chiles from the Fourth Division, a regiment of infantry under Colonel James P. Saunders from the Fifth Division, a regiment of cavalry under Lieutenant Colonel Redman Wilfley from the Fifth Division, a battalion of cavalry under Lieutenant Colonel John R. Boyd from the Fifth Division that included Captain E.V. Kelly's artillery battery, and perhaps one or two other small units. The total force numbered about 2,500.[1]

The State Guard force reached the crossing of the Missouri River at Blue Mills Landing about six miles south of Liberty late in the afternoon of September 16, and the troops began crossing the river on three small flatboats. The artillerymen were among the first to cross, and Kelly planted his battery on the south side commanding the crossing. Colonel Chiles's cavalry was stationed as a rear guard about two miles south of Liberty on the road to the landing while the rest of the troops crossed. Even though the river was fairly narrow at the landing, the crossing of 2,500 men and one hundred wagons of supplies required considerable time, and it continued all night without interruption. On the morning of the seventeenth, a large number of the state troops, including Patton's infantry and Chiles's cavalry, had still not crossed.[2]

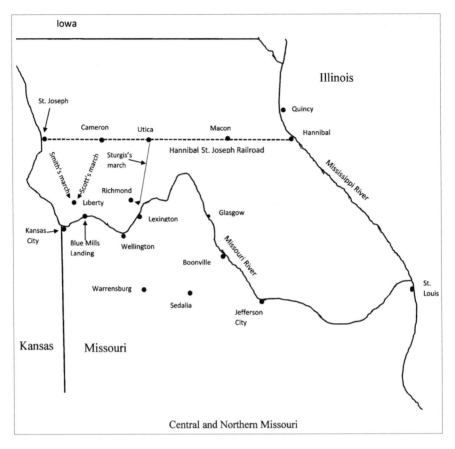

Map showing locations pertinent to the Battle of Blue Mills Landing and to the Union efforts to reinforce Lexington. *Drawn by the author.*

Meanwhile, Colonel Scott reached the Liberty area about 7:00 a.m. the same morning and went into camp just north of town to wait for Colonel Smith, who had been bogged down by heavy rains. About 11:00 a.m., Scott's advance guard encountered Chiles's cavalry along the road to the landing and received a sharp fire that drove them back with a loss of four men killed and one wounded, while the Southerners suffered no casualties. Scott's advance retreated to camp with the news of their misfortune, and Scott sent word back to Smith beseeching him "to hasten his command." In the meantime, Scott decided to push forward with only his small force of about 560 men to try to delay or disrupt the Missouri State Guard crossing.[3]

About two miles south of Liberty, Scott met and drove in the State Guard pickets, but the Rebel retreat was a mere ruse. At mid-afternoon about two miles from the landing, the Federals came upon Patton's infantry concealed in the woods on both sides of the road and in a dry creek bed. The Missouri troops, according to Scott, "opened a heavy fire which drove back our skirmishers and made simultaneous attacks upon our front and right."[4]

When the Federals returned the initial fire, a brief panic ensued, according to a soldier in Patton's regiment, among the raw State Guard recruits, who "had never heard the wiz of a minnie [sic] ball before." Steeling their nerves, the Southerners, however, quickly opened such a "dreadful volley of musketry," as the Liberty Tribune called it, that several of the Federal cannoneers were killed or wounded after getting off only two shots, and Scott's six-pounder was left without enough artillerists to man it. Grabbing the matches and primer so that the cannon would not be of immediate use to the enemy, the remaining gunners beat a hasty retreat, abandoning the artillery piece.[5]

The fight lasted about an hour before, in Colonel Scott's words, "it was deemed advisable to fall back," and he began what he called a slow retreat toward Liberty, checking the Missouri State Guard pursuit with return fire. Some of the men of the Third Iowa were able to retrieve the six-pounder, pulling it off by hand, but the ammunition wagon became lodged between a stump and a tree and had to be abandoned.[6]

David R. Atchison, who had been dispatched by Price from Lexington to Liberty to hasten the reinforcements from northwest Missouri, put a different slant on the Federal retreat. A former U.S. senator and now a general in the Missouri State Guard, Atchison reported, "The Federal troops almost immediately fled, our men pursuing rapidly, shooting them down until they annihilated the rear of their army." Atchison admitted that the Federals attempted to make a stand two or three times but immediately ran after firing a single volley each time. "Our men followed them like hounds on a wolf chase, strewing the road with dead and wounded."[7]

In the fight at Blue Mills Landing, the Federals lost about eighteen to twenty killed and about fifty to sixty wounded. The State Guard, on the other hand, suffered comparatively light casualties, with perhaps two or three killed and fifteen to twenty wounded.[8]

After Scott's retreat to Liberty, Smith finally came into camp with his cavalry shortly after dark, and his infantry arrived a couple hours later. Because his men were fatigued by the march and he was leery about launching a night assault on an enemy that was reportedly entrenched, Smith postponed a movement until morning. After daylight on the eighteenth, the combined force marched back to the landing but found that the last of the Missouri troops had crossed at about

David R. Atchison arrived at Liberty from Lexington in time for the Battle of Blue Mills Landing. *Courtesy of the Library of Congress.*

3:00 a.m. After Smith had left St. Joseph, a runner had been dispatched to him to deliver General Pope's instructions to continue to Lexington from Liberty, but the messenger had inexplicably returned to St. Joseph without having overtaken Smith's command. Thus, the Federals at Liberty now began marching back toward St. Joseph without attempting to relieve Mulligan.[9]

After completing their crossing of the river on September 17 and in the early morning of September 18, the State Guard troops from northwest Missouri marched for Wellington, seven miles west of Lexington. Many of them went into camp there on the evening of the eighteenth, while some of the forces leading the advance were hurried forward to Price's camp.[10]

Meanwhile, at Lexington, September 17, the day of the Blue Mills fight, passed much as the sixteenth had, with almost constant skirmishing between the pickets but little else of import happening. Preparing in earnest to lay siege to the Federal position, Price sent in another flag of truce on the morning of the seventeenth warning the Federals that they had three hours to vacate the fortifications or else be driven out, but Mulligan again declined the invitation to leave. The same day, the Missourians released twelve Union men who had been confined as prisoners, and a Federal officer managed to slip out with them and make his way to the college fortifications, bringing word to Lieutenant McClure and his comrades that the Southern troops planned "to eat breakfast with us tomorrow morning." Undaunted by the threat, McClure, who had been expecting a State Guard assault for several days, was simply glad that it had once again been postponed, giving the Federals additional time to work on their fortifications. "This day's work adds just so much more to our strength," he told his diary.[11]

Price also spread the word among the townspeople of Lexington on the seventeenth advising them to temporarily abandon their homes. Many women and children took refuge at the houses of friends and relatives in the surrounding countryside, but Susan McCausland, eager to witness the coming contest, was among the plucky women who refused to budge.[12]

Upon the arrival of his ordnance train on or about the seventeenth, Price handed out ten rounds of ammunition to the soldiers who previously had none, and his initial maneuvering to invest the college grounds might have begun on the seventeenth as well. However, little significant movement occurred until the following day. Sixty or seventy loads of baled hemp were also brought into Lexington on the seventeenth. The hemp was destined to play an important role in the coming siege of the college fortifications.[13]

Chapter 7

THE SIEGE OF LEXINGTON

Day One

Reveille sounded before daylight in the Missouri State Guard camp on the morning of September 18, and orders were given for the troops to prepare to move out. After taking breakfast, they gathered at the fairgrounds shortly after sunrise and took up the line of march toward Lexington with their "colors flying and a full band of field music in front." Advancing about a half mile, the head of the column paused to give the troops in the rear time to form and close ranks. As the march resumed, it split into two columns, one veering west to approach the town along a road nearer the river (i.e. Thirteenth Street) while the other continued along the main road (i.e. Twentieth Street) into Lexington.[1]

The beat of the drums and the cheering of the state troops as they marched along sounded the alarm at the Union fortifications a mile or more away. "Hark! I hear their cheering and their drums beating," Lieutenant McClure wrote in his diary at 7:00 a.m. "Now they cheer again. Do they expect to terrify us with the sound of their fifteen thousand voices?"[2]

Nearing the Union outposts, the State Guard band members from the various regiments fell out of ranks and formed at the side of the road to invigorate the march with lively tunes. "Here the air resounded with bursts of martial music; 'the ear-piercing fife, the doubling drum,' gave forth their notes of war," remembered Ephraim Anderson, "and the ranks moved on in a lively step."[3]

Colonel Mulligan watched the State Guard approach from behind his fortifications: "They came as one dark, moving mass, their polished guns gleaming in the sunlight, their banners waving, and their drums

Colonel James Mulligan. *Courtesy of the Library of Congress.*

beating—everywhere, as far as we could see were men, men, men—approaching grandly." As the Southerners got nearer, the Union soldiers stood quiet and solemn behind their breastworks, according to Mulligan, and "as Father Butler went around among them they asked his blessing and received it uncovered: then turned and sternly cocked their muskets."[4]

The Federal pickets retreated with little resistance before the massive State Guard advance, and the cheering of Price's army was echoed by that of the townspeople as the men marched into Lexington. "The ladies greeted us warmly," recalled Anderson. "Many of them came out, and, assembling in groups, cheered on the men, while others were dispensing water to the command."[5]

Susan McCausland was one of the ladies cheering on the Southern soldiers. In fact, she later recalled, as she was viewing the proceedings from the front porch of her father's home, she was "so radiantly glad of events that a galloping Federal picket on the run my way resented it to the extent of reining in his horse to fire upon me." Luckily for Susan, her sister was nearby and threw herself on Susan, knocking her to floor as the bullet whizzed above their heads.[6]

It was about 9:00 a.m. by the time the first of the State Guard units formed at the locations they had been assigned surrounding the Union fortifications. Parsons's division took its position lining Main Street (i.e. North Street) to

The building where Price had his headquarters as it appears today. *Photo by the author.*

66

the east of its intersection with Eleventh Street, where the courthouse sat, and Colonel Congreve Jackson's division supported Parsons in front of and to the west of the courthouse, while General Price set up his headquarters in a second-floor room of a nearby building. Curious spectators came out to view the proceedings, and Lieutenant Barlow recalled the air of tense excitement among the townspeople. "The street was lined with ladies, sobbing and waving their handkerchief and one old gentleman mounted a gate post and 'exhorted' our marching column in true camp-meeting style."[7]

Susan McCausland was probably one of the women Barlow remembered who lined the street to greet him and his fellow soldiers. "By the middle of the forenoon of Wednesday, the 18th," she recalled,

> *the stars and bars floating within the city limits, and the strains of Dixie came ringing clear through the gold of the perfect day. I needed to go but a single square from my father's residence…to look up the extent of Main street, and this I did so soon as I caught the sound of Dixie. What I saw there was an army without any pretense of uniform of any kind, but moving in orderly precision into some determined-upon position. This was Gen. Parson's line, drawn along Main street.*[8]

As Susan stood at the corner of Main and Broadway watching the proceedings, a friend of hers in Price's army, Lieutenant Charley Wallace, came along and questioned why she was out in the open. "You would better go to shelter at once," he warned, "as we are about to fight, right away." The admonition, however, merely spurred the daring young woman to seek a more advantageous position from which to view the unfolding drama.[9]

Barlow and his comrades were somewhat less eager about the prospect of battle than their bellicose exhorter, and it took something other than "Dixie" to stay their qualms. Barlow recalled that Price's brass band, under cover at the foot of a hill that Main Street overlooked, struck up a lively Irish battle tune called "Garryowen" that seemed to allay the fears of Parsons's infantry and artillery, many of them Irishmen from St. Louis, about going into combat.[10]

General Price ordered Parsons and his men to take the hill in front of them, where the Federal pickets were strongly posted, and Parsons sent Guibor's battery and a company of skirmishers under Captain Champion to the front to carry out the order. Lieutenant Barlow described the ensuing action:

> *Up the hill we went with two guns, the infantry charging on each side, all in a scramble and all together, meeting a tolerably hot fire, but not the*

General Mosby M. Parsons's brigade was stationed along and north of Main Street during most of the siege. *Mosby Parsons Uncased, #30260, in the collection of Wilson's Creek National Battlefield. Courtesy of the National Park Service.*

murderous fusillade which was expected. Our infantry opened fire, our two guns were formed "action front"; a negro woman with a white baby went flying across the street under fire, and Jack Murphy sent a solid shot bang through a brick residence close on our left.[11]

Many women and children of Lexington had already vacated their homes and retired to safer confines in the country, and many of those who remained sought the refuge of cellars and similar hiding places when the first fighting broke out. However, Mrs. McCausland and the black woman with the baby weren't the only ladies who dared to expose themselves to the fire. During the initial assault on the Union fortifications, according to Ephraim Anderson, the women of Lexington seemed "to regard the cannon balls and shells from the enemy's mortars less than we did ourselves."[12]

Inside the earthworks, Lieutenant McClure grew pensive as the battle began in earnest. "Now I must cease writing for the present," he wrote in his diary. "I am almost certain that we will achieve a victory, but I may have to lay down my life. It is a mournful thought to entertain, but I look calmly upon death."[13]

Lieutenant Barlow was wounded during the charge up the hill but not enough to render him incapable of noting the outcome of Parsons's initial attack: "The enemy instantly gave way, not being in force, we quietly followed, invested the fort and opened a slow fire."[14]

After driving in the pickets, Parsons established his battery on Cedar Street (i.e. Eleventh) north of Main within about five hundred yards of the Federal fortifications. Colonel Joseph Kelly's infantry regiment supported the battery on the right, and Colonel C.B. Alexander's cavalry was stationed to the left of the battery. Colonel Robert McCulloch's cavalry was placed to the rear of the battery, while Jackson's division, maintaining its position on Main Street, was held in reserve. "From this point," said General Parsons, "Capt. Guibor opened a galling fire from his guns upon the enemy's works."[15]

General Rains and his Eighth Division, consisting of slightly over three thousand men, reached downtown Lexington about the same time as Parsons and took up a position north and east of

General James S. Rains's brigade was stationed in a semicircular position east of the Masonic College throughout the siege. *General James S. Rains, #30038, in the collection of Wilson's Creek National Battlefield. Courtesy of the National Park Service.*

the college fort in a semicircular line about six to eight hundred yards away. With the Federal pickets largely driven in, the battle now became mostly an artillery duel. Rains opened on the Union earthworks with his two batteries, one stationed east of the college and commanded by nineteen-year-old captain Churchill Clark, grandson of explorer William Clark, and the other, Bledsoe's battery, stationed north of Clark and still commanded by Emmett MacDonald in Bledsoe's absence.[16]

Rains offered a gold medal to any artillerist who could knock down a U.S. flag planted at the southeast corner of the Federal breastworks. The boyish Clark promptly rose to the challenge and won the prize. "I felt a little queer," he later wrote to his aunt, "when I saw the stars and stripes fall by my own hand, but still went on…The way I made the Feds scatter in their trenches was amusing. I did more execution than anyone else. My battery had a good position and tore the college nearly to pieces."[17]

About 11:00 a.m., Rains advanced his men to a protected area within about 350 yards of the Federal entrenchments on the northeast and within about 500 yards on the east. He remained in this position throughout the day, continuing to bang away at the fortifications with his artillery, occasionally throwing out skirmishers and sharpshooters "to annoy the enemy," and guarding a spring to prevent the Federals from getting water.[18]

Arriving in the downtown area with his Second Division at 10:00 a.m., General Harris was greeted, according to a lieutenant commanding one of his companies, by "a big cannon ball coming down the street almost spent but bouncing up and down with a force sufficient to kill a man. I gave the order to file right to left and the ball passed through the Company and hurt no one."[19]

Harris took up a position near Main Street, supporting General Parsons. Seeing Guibor's guns already in action, Harris ordered his own artillery captain, James W. Kneisley, to unlimber at an elevated intersection of two streets nearby and "imitate the movements of the battery of Gen. Parsons' division." At the same time, he sent a company under Captain B.F. Davis, armed with Minié rifles, to act as skirmishers in support of the battery, while the rest of the command was held in reserve behind the protection of houses. Returning Kneisley's artillery fire, the Federals "annoyed" Harris's men with grape and solid shot on one or two occasions, but Harris merely shifted Kneisley's position slightly to an area that afforded better protection. Captain Kneisley continued bombarding the Union fortifications for about an hour, halting his fire, according to Harris, only after his ammunition began to run low and his men exhausted themselves in the excessive heat.[20]

The Fourth Division, commanded by Colonel Benjamin A. Rives in the absence of Brigadier General William Y. Slack and consisting of a regiment of infantry under Colonel John T. Hughes and a regiment of dismounted cavalry under Lieutenant Colonel Louis C. Bohannon, reached the main part of town shortly after Harris. A portion of the Fifth Division, whose commander, Brigadier General Alexander E. Steen, was likewise absent, was also attached to Rives's division during the march to town. Taking up positions as spectators during the "considerable cannonading" between the Federal batteries and those of Guibor and Kneisley, Rives and his men were held in readiness until about 10:30 a.m., when General Price ordered Rives to take a position west of the Union fortifications on a bluff overlooking Oliver Anderson's hemp warehouse with a view toward cutting off Mulligan's access to the river.[21]

Colonel Hughes led the march, filing west along Broadway to the main landing and then following the river downstream toward the Federal fortifications. After proceeding a short distance down the river, Hughes was met by a "sharp fire" from Federals stationed at a steam mill, Morrison's iron foundry, and other buildings in the same vicinity. Returning the fire, Hughes succeeded in driving his attackers from the buildings, but as he continued down the river, other Federals kept up the assault from the bluffs overlooking the riverbank and from the steamboat *Clara Bell* and steam ferryboat *Belle of Lexington*, which were moored along a shelving beach farther downstream.[22]

At this point, General Parsons hurried his artillery guns down Tenth Street toward the river and opened fire on the Federals concealed on the steep hillsides behind houses, piles of lumber, and other hiding places. Stirred by the State Guard cannonade, the Federals on the bluffs dropped back toward the relative security of their entrenchments, and those occupying the steamboats, fearful of being cut off from their fortifications, also absconded to safer ground. Guibor's battery then retreated to the vicinity it had previously occupied, unlimbering this time at the intersection of Third and Tenth. Here the battery, in the words of Lieutenant Barlow, "settled down to regular siege work."[23]

With the Federal skirmishers on the hillside driven back, Colonel Hughes, acting on the orders of Colonel Rives, advanced along the river, commandeered the steamboats, and started back with them to the main landing about three-quarters of a mile upstream. There he turned the boats over to Captain William Merrick, whom Rives had detailed to take charge of them. The *Clara Bell*, which Mulligan had seized less than a week earlier as it was passing on the river, contained a good deal of sugar, salt, coffee, and other supplies, and the Missourians also took a number of Federal horses from the boats or the vicinity of the boats.[24]

General McBride, bringing up the rear of the Missouri State Guard march from the fairgrounds, reached Price's downtown headquarters shortly after Rives had been dispatched to occupy the bluff overlooking the Anderson warehouse. Ordered to support him, McBride sent part of his command to circle the Masonic College on the east and get between the Union fortifications and the river, while another column marched down Broadway to the river on the west side of the fortifications and came upon the rear of Rives's command near the foundry. Discovering that Hughes had already secured the steamboats and that Hughes and Rives were filing off to the right to take possession of the bluff as General Price had directed, McBride's column continued along the riverbank to hook up with the rest of his command and halted so that his line joined Rives's line to encircle the Federal fortifications on the west and northwest. Although Hughes's infantry and Guibor's battery had forced the Federals to fall back, many of their sharpshooters were still hiding on the bluff, including some ensconced on the grounds of the Anderson house, and they kept up a steady fire on the State Guard line as it closed on the Union fortifications. According to Rives, the Federals were even firing from the Anderson house itself, despite the fact that it was being used as a hospital and was flying a white flag.[25]

McBride's command chased the Federals up the northwest bluff of College Hill, "each party keeping up a running fire," according to the general. The Federals discharged two mines at the summit of the bluff, seriously wounding several of McBride's men, as the bluecoats continued to scamper toward their entrenchments. Among the fleeing Federals were two companies under Major Becker that had been detailed to guard the steamboats from a lunette outside the main line of entrenchments. Abandoning the small breastwork, they now, in the words of the 1881 county history, "beat a hasty retreat" toward the main entrenchments. The pursuing Missouri troops captured a U.S. flag that the home guards had abandoned, and they planted a Southern flag in its stead. Then, leaving a force at the brow of the hill, McBride gathered up his wounded and retired to lower ground, from where he dispatched a runner to General Price asking for assistance.[26]

At 11:15 a.m., General Price, having received McBride's request for assistance, ordered General Harris to support General McBride and Colonel Rives and also told him to take possession of the Anderson house if, in Harris's opinion, it could be captured without severe casualties. Leaving his battery under the personal watch of General Price, Harris started down

General James McBride's brigade was positioned northwest of the Union fortifications during the siege. *James H. McBride, #805, in the collection of Wilson's Creek National Battlefield. Courtesy of the National Park Service.*

Tenth Street toward the river, deploying some of his men to the right to crawl up the steep hillside southwest of the Anderson house and fire at any of the Federals who might expose themselves above their breastworks.[27]

When Harris reached a point along Tenth due west of the Anderson house, where a carriageway that served as the property's only access road was located, he dismounted and climbed the hill on the opposite side of Tenth, the bluff occupied by Colonel Rives, to get a better view of the house and surrounding grounds. "From a personal inspection of the position occupied by the hospital," Harris said, "I became satisfied that it was invaluable to me as a point of annoyance and mask for my approach to the enemy." At the same time, he received a message that General Price had conducted his own reconnaissance of the hospital through a field glass and likewise concluded that it occupied a strategic position. Therefore, Harris, consulting with Rives, promptly ordered an assault on the Anderson house. Angry because the Federals had supposedly been firing at him from a house they were using as a hospital, Rives enthusiastically seconded Harris's decision.[28]

About noon, a company in Rives's division under the command of Lieutenant F.G. Bransford, supported by the cavalry regiments of Lieutenant Colonel E.B. Hull and Major G.B. Milton from Harris's division, carried out the order, storming the Anderson house and taking possession of it with little or no resistance. After securing the building, Bransford's men found, in addition to over one hundred sick and wounded Federal soldiers, a number of escaped slaves hidden in the cellar. They turned the slaves over to Rives, who caused them to be returned under guard to their owners in the

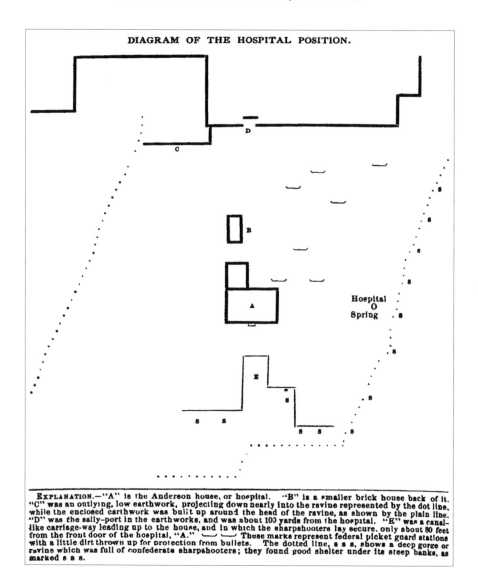

Map of the Anderson house position. *From the* History of Lafayette County.

surrounding countryside, some as far away as Utica. Surgeon Wyatt claimed that a number of mulatto girls who had been held prisoner and raped almost to the point of death by Union soldiers were found on this day as well, but if they were among the slaves held in the cellar, Rives did not say so.[29]

Leaving a small force of men to augment Rives in holding the Anderson house, Harris descended the hill and found that the left wing of his command under Colonel Martin Green had joined forces with McBride and was now occupying a position in common with McBride. Harris ordered Green to file to the left and take up a position to the left of McBride, extending the State Guard line along the river. He then ordered the rest of his command to move to the support of Green's left, further extending the line to the north of the Masonic College, so that Harris's left nearly reached Rains's right and the Federal fortifications were now almost entirely surrounded.[30]

As the battle raged on the college grounds and the surrounding streets, many Lexington homes, by midday of the eighteenth, had been turned into makeshift hospitals to treat the wounded Missouri soldiers. "It must have been that the first volleys from the intrenchments did deadly work," Susan McCausland recalled, "for not long after the opening roar of the guns, men crimsoned by war's red touch began to be borne to places of shelter. Private houses were opened to receive them, and in some instances limbs were amputated on dining tables, on parlor floors, and in one case an arm was removed while the owner lay stretched on the top of a piano."[31]

The firing of musketry and artillery continued throughout the day. "Fast and furious bombs and balls hurtled and screeched into the citadel and from there into town," Mrs. McCausland remembered. "On this first afternoon the bombardment was so heavy the thunder of the guns was heard at Carrollton, thirty miles away."[32]

Many Lexington residents like Susan McCausland viewed the action from such up-close vantages that they became supporting actors in the riveting theater as it unfolded on their home stage, while curious spectators from miles around also flocked into town to watch the high drama. Those north of the Missouri River, however, had to content themselves with viewing the performance from afar. "There were thousands of persons—men, women, and children—from the neighboring counties, gathered on the banks of the river opposite Lexington all day Wednesday," said one Union report, "watching with intense eagerness the programme of the battle."[33]

Some of those who flocked into Lexington after the battle opened did more than just watch. "Old men and boys gathered from the surrounding counties with arms in their hands," according to the county history, "and crept up and took a pop or two at the 'Yankees' in the breastworks. Indeed, men of all ages, citizens, not soldiers, did the same. Many men brought their wives with them to see the 'sport' of a battle. Some of the visitors rode in carriages, and the occasion seemed to be regarded as a sort of pic-nic, or holiday affair."[34]

One old Texan, according to a Union correspondent to the *St. Louis Missouri Republican*, took his paramilitary role more seriously than most.

"Dressed in buckskin and armed with a long rifle," he showed up in the early morning carrying a dinner pail. "Taking a good position, he banged away at the Federals till noon, then rested an hour, ate his dinner after which he resumed operations until six p.m. when he returned home to supper and a night's sleep." The next morning at seven o'clock he came back similarly outfitted and armed to "begin his regular day's work," and he repeated the routine again on the third and final day of the siege.[35]

The State Guard's continual bombardment of the Federal fortifications throughout the day on Wednesday, according to a Union newspaper report, did little damage in terms of human casualties, but it "tore great limbs from the trees, opened many huge chasms in the beautiful college building, and quite as frequently as otherwise, the big balls went whizzing harmlessly over the Federal works, and dropped somewhere in the very places occupied by the Confederate forces, with a result best known to themselves."[36]

After taking possession of the Anderson house, Colonel Rives filled it with his sharpshooters, who, according to a Union newspaper report, "clambered up on the roof, got behind the chimneys, fired from the windows, doorways, cistern—any thing that would afford them protection." The newspaper correspondent reported that the firing of the Missouri sharpshooters so annoyed the Federals that Mulligan determined to retake the building, and Rives, in his after-action report, concurred with that assessment.[37]

However, the firing of the sharpshooters was hardly the only thing about the Anderson house episode that annoyed Colonel Mulligan. Informed shortly after noon that the building had been taken by the enemy, Mulligan grew irate that Price's troops had dared to assault a hospital. "I had supposed," he later wrote, "that the little white flag was a sufficient protection for the wounded and dying soldier who had finished his service and who was powerless for harm."[38]

Seething with anger, Mulligan wanted to retake the hospital immediately, but he had trouble finding a company that was up to the task. Captain George Hoge of Peabody's regiment led a sortie to retake the building but was quickly driven back, and a company of home guards balked at even attempting the dangerous mission. With a minor mutiny on his hands, Mulligan turned to Captain Michael Gleeson, commanding the Montgomery Guard, a prewar militia unit that became part of the Irish Brigade. Gleeson rose to the occasion, Mulligan later recalled with admiration, admonishing his men "that they were called upon to go where the others dared not" and imploring them "to uphold the gallant name which they bore."[39]

According to one report, a "German company" belonging to Peabody's command was one of the companies that refused to undertake the task. However, this was an error, according to Major Van Horn, who said that the so-called German company under Captain Joseph Schmitz joined the Montgomery Guards in their charge. It might be, instead, that Schmitz's company was among the men led by Captain Hoge.[40]

In any case, as Major Van Horn later observed, the undertaking was a "desperate venture," since at least one hundred yards of open ground lay between the Federal fortifications and the Anderson house. It was about two or three o'clock when the word to charge was given, and the Union soldiers, in Mulligan's words, "started at first quick, then double quick, then on the run, then faster—still the deadly drift of lead poured upon them, but on they went—a wild line of steel, and what is better than steel, irresistible human will."[41]

Susan McCausland watched the charge from her vantage on Third Street overlooking the Anderson house and grounds. "A double line of human forms," she said, "appeared on top of the embankment, rushed over, followed by the serried ranks of others, all firing upon the house as they hurtled down upon it. And how they fell! some of them, on the way, and lay there amongst the flowers of the garden…And how they yelled as they charged! It was a daring and brilliant sortie."[42]

Private Palmer, although not a member of the Montgomery Guards, was at the outer entrenchments when the Guards "came along on the run" after the order to charge had been given, and he voluntarily joined the attack. "We reached into the building and drove the enemy from the lower floor," said Palmer, "some of them running toward the river and some running up the stairs. They kept up a fire from the upper story and from the direction of the River so that many were killed and wounded of our party."[43]

After getting possession of the lower floor, the Federals realized their mission was only half complete because the Missouri State Guard still held the second floor. Furthermore, Captain Gleeson, who had been seriously wounded in the dash across the Anderson property, was no longer able to command. The remaining officers tried to get the men to charge up the stairway, but no one wanted to take the lead. Seeing their hesitancy, Palmer, who described himself as "filled with dash and enthusiasm," ran forward and jumped onto the second step of the stairway. Turning to the Montgomery Guards, he shouted that if they would follow him, he would lead them. They cheered and came rushing forward. "And on we went with a yell and a rush," Palmer recalled.[44]

George H. Palmer led the charge to retake the Anderson house. *Courtesy of the Battle of Lexington State Historic Site.*

Upstairs, the Federals found all the doors to the rooms closed. Bashing in one of the doors, Palmer saw four Missouri soldiers huddled in the room. He yelled for them to surrender, and although two of them made a start to raise their weapons, all four quickly complied when the Federals accompanying Palmer appeared behind him. The men with Palmer cursed and threatened to kill the captives, but he managed to protect them and started marching them down the stairs.[45]

Incensed by the number of their fellow soldiers who had been killed in storming the hospital, some of the Montgomery Guards on the first floor immediately rushed the State Guard captives and shot three of them to death when they appeared on the stairway. The fourth captive was William Mansur, a member of Lieutenant Bransford's company, which had taken the hospital earlier in the day. He was in the rear as the prisoners were being marched down the stairway, and upon seeing his fellow soldiers being executed, he turned and ran back upstairs. However, he was met immediately by a Federal soldier, who started marching him at the point of a bayonet back down the stairs toward the firing squad. Partway down the stairs, Mansur suddenly turned, deflected his guard's bayonet, and leaped over the stair railing into a hallway. He dashed down the hallway into a side room, where he was met by another irate Federal. As the soldier raised his weapon to kill Mansur, an Irishman known to Mansur only as Brown or Bowen intervened and, together with a comrade, escorted the prisoner to the lockup.[46]

According to Mansur, two other Missouri soldiers, besides Mansur and his three companions, were also upstairs at the time the Federals stormed the second floor. One, a captain named Barger, escaped by making himself known as a Mason to a wounded Federal soldier and fellow Mason, who allowed Barger to crawl in bed with him and pretend to be a hospital patient. The sixth man upstairs, Henry Queener, who was Colonel Rives's cook, simply hid out in the house and eventually managed to escape.[47]

The Union troops held the Anderson house for only about an hour before the State Guard determined to retake it. Robert Armstrong, a Union soldier who had been wounded during the Federal assault on the house and was forced to stay behind as a hospital patient, described what happened when the Rebels mounted their charge: "We made an attempt to retreat, but found that they had thrown out a force from the other side and that we were surrounded.

Top: William Mansur, one of the Missourians trapped in the Anderson house after the Union retook the building. *Courtesy of the Battle of Lexington State Historic Site.*

Right: Staircase inside the Anderson house appearing today much as it did when Mansur leaped over the railing to escape the Union bayonets. *Photo by the author.*

The fighting was terrible for a few minutes, when a company under Captain Smith made a charge from the works and opened a gap that let our side out, and they left, taking all the wounded they could with them."[48]

Armstrong, who had lost a lot of blood from a wound in the arm, added, "I stayed and faced what I supposed would be death." Instead of killing Armstrong, however, the Southerners who stormed the building "seemed to be in a good humor" and simply made fun of him, asking whether his mother knew he was out, and the officers who came in shortly afterward also treated him kindly.[49]

A good portion of the Union's total casualties for the entire siege occurred during the Federals' assault on the hospital on the eighteenth and the State Guard's retaking of the building later the same day. Colonel Mulligan said that only thirty-five of the eighty "lions" who went out at midafternoon came back two hours later and that the remaining forty-five were left strewn "upon the field of death." This might have been a slight exaggeration, but other sources confirm that the Montgomery Guards alone lost as many as twenty-five or thirty in killed and wounded. One of the Union wounded was Father Butler, whose forehead was grazed by a stray bullet.[50]

The Anderson house episode remained a controversial subject long after the Civil War ended. Northerners maintained that the Missouri troops had violated a fundamental convention of war by assaulting an unfortified building that was being used as a hospital and was displaying a white flag. Former State Guard soldiers, however, adamantly claimed that Union sharpshooters had fired on them from the cover of the Anderson house. This claim was just as adamantly denied by Union observers like Dr. Franklin Cooley, a Lexington physician who was in the hospital serving as a Federal surgeon at the time the Missourians took possession of it. As is often the case with disputes in which the opposing views are so divergent, the truth in this matter probably lies somewhere in the middle, and a friendly court of inquiry into the hospital matter in 1872 concluded as much. It is likely, as Dr. Cooley and others claimed, that the Union soldiers did not actually fire from the Anderson house, but they probably fired from such proximity to it that the fire could easily have been mistaken as having come from the house. Also, by situating a hospital in a strategic location in the middle of a battlefield, the Federals forfeited any reasonable expectation that the building would not become a military target. In fact, General Harris's after-action report suggests that General Price ordered the taking of the Anderson house because of its strategic location. The claim that Union soldiers had fired from the building might have been, at least to some extent, tacked on as an additional justification for the action.[51]

The actions that occurred on the premises of the hospital were no less controversial than Price's initial decision to take possession of it. There appears to be no evidence to support the Union claim that the state troops wantonly shot and bayoneted Federal soldiers upon initially taking possession of the building. Instead, the Anderson house was taken with very little resistance, and if Union soldier Robert Armstrong is to be believed, the Federal hospital patients were treated kindly by the State Guard. As for the Union soldiers' killing of the three Missouri troops after they had already surrendered, one can say only that, while such an action is not excusable, it is certainly understandable given the fact that the enraged Federals had just seen many of their comrades mowed down during their dash from the entrenchments, some of them presumably shot by the same Southern soldiers who now sought protection as prisoners.

Colonel Mulligan was infuriated not only by the State Guard's decision to storm the Anderson house in the first place but also by what happened, or rather what didn't happen, after the Missourians took final possession of it. Mulligan was forced to set up another hospital in the college dormitory, but Father Butler and Dr. William Winer, official surgeon of the Irish Brigade, were held at the Anderson house, according to Mulligan, "against all rules of war." Winer was not allowed to return to the fortifications to treat the sick and wounded there, and because of his absence, Captain David Moriarty of the Irish Brigade, who had been a physician in civilian life, was forced to "lay aside his sword and go into the hospital." The only surgeon's instrument available to Moriarty, according to Mulligan, was a razor, and this shortage of physician's tools compounded the terrible suffering of the wounded men inside the hospital.[52]

Mulligan's indignant outrage over Dr. Winer's being held prisoner "against all rules of war" seems a bit dissimulating. It's quite possible that Winer remained at the Anderson house at least somewhat voluntarily to treat the wounded there because that is where most of the Federal wounded were located. In addition, Dr. Winer and Father Butler were held for only a matter of hours, as they were allowed to return to the fortifications the next day.[53]

While the action around the hospital was unfolding, General Price continued to maneuver his troops into position. At midafternoon, a battalion of Colonel Jackson's reserves was dispatched to the levee to guard the boats that had been captured earlier in the day. Later in the evening, Price sent a portion of Steen's Fifth Division to support Colonel

Rives and General Harris west and northwest of the college fort. This included Captain Kelly's battery, which had been hurried forward after the action at Blue Mills Landing.[54]

Shortly before dark on the eighteenth, two of Kelly's guns were lugged up the hill northwest of the college where the lunette that the Union home guards had abandoned earlier in the day was located. The Missouri State Guard soldiers were in the process of planting the guns at the lunette when approximately two hundred Union soldiers, led personally by Colonel Mulligan, made a charge to retake the position. Mulligan "led with a shout," according to the *Chicago Times*, "his sword waving high in the air, and his tall form springing over the ground like an antelope. The men pressed on with shouts and fairly precipitated themselves headlong into the trench." They drove the Missouri soldiers out of the lunette and down the slope, captured the Rebel flag previously planted at or near the lunette, and momentarily took charge of the State Guard artillery pieces. The Missourians, however, rallied and retook the guns, driving the Federals toward their entrenchments.[55]

Less effusive in his language than the *Times* correspondent, General McBride said about this action only that the Federals "raised the shout" about dark "and charged within a short distance of the brow of the bluff" but were "quickly repulsed."[56]

After the skirmish, the State Guard soldiers took their guns and retired to lower ground, and the Federals momentarily abandoned the small, outer breastwork as well, retiring to within their entrenchments to show off the captured Rebel flag. Lieutenant McClure described the flag as "a singular-looking thing; it has a blue field with fifteen stars, then one broad stripe of red, then one of white, and another red one, but three stripes in all." (This was a description of the Confederate Stars and Bars, except that the official Confederate flag never had as many as fifteen stars.)[57]

On the evening of the eighteenth, Federal soldiers also made a sally on the east side of the fortifications, which General Rains quickly repulsed, but the siege mostly settled into the firing of sharpshooters and cannoneers. Martha Vivian, who lived east of Lexington, could hear the firing from several miles away, and after the war, she recalled the sounds on the night of the eighteenth: "The shots were about as fast as popcorn in a skillet and, above these, could be heard the roar of cannon as though the whole world were falling to pieces."[58]

Newspaperman Franc Wilkie, who was traveling with General Sturgis north of the river on the eighteenth, heard the sounds as well. "All that day, with scarcely a moment's cessation," he reported, "there came to our ears a duet of tenore winds and basso thunderings that seemed to shake the solid foundations of the earth." Now, camped that night fifteen miles from Lexington, Wilkie could "hear with startling distinctness the incessant war of the conflict, and during every instant from the morning of Wednesday till 2 o'clock of the morning of Thursday, there seemed to be a tremendous thunder-storm playing on the verge of the horizon."[59]

Back in Lexington, as darkness settled over the town, Susan McCausland was struck by the surreal scene wrought by the guns of war: "The night which closed this sad day was a lurid one. Hot shell from the citadel had set on fire some frame houses in town, and huge columns of smoke and flame luridly purpled the sky and turned the world into a place of strange horrors."[60]

Chapter 8

THE SIEGE OF LEXINGTON

Day Two

The fighting opened on the morning of the nineteenth mainly as a contest between sharpshooters, and the trend continued throughout the day. "Thursday the cannonade amounted to but little," a Union correspondent told the *St. Louis Missouri Republican*. "But the cracking of small-arms was incessant; and so thick and close were the enemy about the works, and so accurate the aim of the sharpshooters, that a man, a head, or a cap shown for a single instant above the works, was sure to be saluted with fifty balls that never went many inches from the mark."[1]

Years after the war, both Susan McCausland and the author of the county history described the fighting on September 19 in similar terms as the *Missouri Republican* correspondent. The county historian said that the owners of old squirrel guns "were getting in their work," firing "at every animated object they saw inside of Mulligan's works." Mrs. McCausland, whose family fed a number of State Guard officers at her home on the morning of the nineteenth, recalled that some of the Southern sharpshooters climbed up trees to get a better vantage, and she surmised, "This practice must have been more galling to the besieged than had been the cannonading."[2]

Indeed, many of the Federals behind the breastworks, including Lieutenant McClure, found the small arms fire of the State Guard troops at least as annoying as their cannonading. "They have many sharpshooters," McClure told his diary early on the morning of the nineteenth, "who have placed themselves round in convenient places; some in trees, others behind stumps and logs, and from their secure position keep constantly firing upon us." Mulligan's sharpshooters occasionally returned the fire, but with little effect, McClure lamented, because the concealed State Guard marksmen were hard to locate.[3]

However, McClure and his Union comrades inside the fortifications soon became used to the constant annoyance of the State Guard sharpshooters. "The rifle and musket balls have been whizzing round our heads so much that we don't notice them as much as we would a bumble bee at home," the lieutenant wrote. He picked up the first couple of balls that struck the ground near him, but he soon concluded that if he picked up every ball that passed over his head so close that he could feel its hiss, he would be loaded down.[4]

Colonel Hughes's infantrymen were among the State Guard sharpshooters McClure and his comrades had to contend with. "On the morning of the 19th," Hughes reported, "we arose from our bivouac upon the hills to renew the attack. This day we continued the fighting vigorously all day, holding possession of the hospital building."[5]

Although the bombardment tapered off on the nineteenth, the cannonading that continued became more strategic. Nineteen-year-old Churchill Clark, who had moved one of the guns of his battery to a position on Sixteenth Street near Franklin Street facing the front of the Masonic College, hit upon the idea of firing hot shot at the college to try to set it on fire. He procured some undersized shot from General Rains's ordnance officer, Colonel John F. Snyder, and heated them until they were red hot in a makeshift forge he had rigged up near his six-pound gun, which was aimed at the Masonic symbol on the wooden gable at the front of the college. "The hot shot then dropped into the cannon," explained Snyder, "on contact with the powder was instantly sent out again on its mission. The young officer sighted his gun well. Several balls going through the gable struck the rafters and fell to the floor below, as we calculated they would."[6]

What Clark had not counted on, however, was the vigilance of the Union defenders inside the college. A Union sharpshooter stationed on the second floor informed Major Van Horn that hot shot was being used against them, and hurrying to the scene, Van Horn grabbed a shovel, scooped up a smoldering cannonball that had fallen to the floor, and tossed the fiery shot out the window. A fifteen-year-old lad named Charles Lantheaume standing nearby volunteered to take over the task and, according to Van Horn, continued cheerfully throwing the shot out as long as they continued to be fired.[7]

Part of the reason that the bombardment slackened on the nineteenth was that both sides began to run low on cannonballs. In order to conserve

Captain Churchill Clark vowed to knock down the Masonic College with his artillery. *Missouri History Museum, St. Louis.*

ammunition, according to Lieutenant Barlow of Guibor's battery, "Each side commenced hunting up those received and sending them back. Many shot were sent back and forth three or four times each, as we discovered by observing their polished sides, made by penetrating earth or brick walls."[8]

The previous day, Southern partisans had intercepted a Union runner bearing a message for Colonel Mulligan that General Sturgis was approaching Lexington north of the Missouri River with reinforcements, and the messenger and his dispatch were turned over to General Price. On the morning of the nineteenth, Price ordered General Parsons's division and Colonel Jackson's division across the river to head off the threat. Parsons and Jackson ferried across with at least three thousand men and marched out about a mile north of the river, where Parsons, in his own words, "ascertained that the enemy had heard of my approach and retired in confusion, leaving 200 of their tents upon the road." Ephraim Anderson, a member of Jackson's command, recalled that the State Guard scouts skirmished briefly with Sturgis's advance, but if such an encounter occurred, it must have been very brief. Neither Parsons nor Jackson mentioned such a skirmish, and Franc Wilkie, the newspaperman with Sturgis, also reported no engagement. Sturgis had learned from an elderly black man that Price had seized the ferryboats at Lexington and sent three thousand troops across the river to meet him, and according to Wilkie, he deemed it "sheer folly to march his meager force into a hornet's nest so formidable in size." Instead, Sturgis left the road he was on and struck off for Richmond, the seat of Ray County, with a view toward forming a junction with Colonel Smith, who was supposed to be marching from St. Joseph. The

next day, however, Sturgis continued his retreat, fearful that Price was marching to cut him off. "So we did not relieve Mulligan," recalled a Union surgeon accompanying Sturgis, "but we were glad to get away ourselves."[9]

After learning that Sturgis had turned back, Parsons recrossed the river about noon and formed his line on the north side of Main Street west of Sixteenth Street (i.e. College Street) facing the college fort. A column of his command attempted an assault on the Federal works but was quickly repulsed. Still, his skirmishers were able to advance to within 150 yards of the fortifications and establish themselves

Samuel M. Sturgis aborted his attempt to relieve Mulligan at Lexington. *Courtesy of the Library of Congress.*

across Sixteenth and along Clinton Street to the west. From here, according to Parsons, they "kept up a murderous fire upon the enemy as they would show themselves upon the entrenchments."[10]

Meanwhile, Colonel Jackson lingered north of the river for about an hour to make sure Sturgis had, in fact, turned back. He then recrossed the river and took up a position in support of Parsons, east of Sixteenth Street and within about 450 yards of the college building, but his men continued to be held in reserve. The regiment of Colonel Robert S. Bevier, which was part of Jackson's command, was among the State Guard forces not actively engaged in the action at Lexington. According to Bevier, "Lying around on the pavement in the shade, dodging the flying brick when struck from some corner wall by a passing shot, and listening to the shrieks of some nervous women, constituted the occupation of my command."[11]

Price continued maneuvering his troops on the nineteenth to dispose them in the most advantageous locations surrounding the Federal fortifications. General Harris moved a battalion under Colonel Edward C. McDonald to the extreme left of his line to perfect his junction with General Rains so that Missouri troops now completely encircled the college fort. Lieutenant Colonel John R. Boyd's battalion of infantry, which had taken part in the affair at Blue Mills Landing, arrived and took up a position around the courthouse, and Captain Kelly's battery was recalled from its assignment north of the fortifications and brought back downtown to support Boyd.[12]

Among the men in Boyd's command were Caldwell and Sam Dunlap, the brothers from Buchanan County who had been captured in June while marching to join Price's army and made to swear allegiance to the Union. They had since renounced the oath and joined the Missouri State Guard after all. Boyd's battalion had spent the night near Wellington, and early on the morning of the nineteenth, a messenger from General Price had come into Boyd's camp, according to Sam Dunlap, with "an order, or rather a request...for all who wished to take a part in the battle of Lexington to come forward and report for duty as infantry immediately."[13]

Other State Guard reinforcements continued to pour in as well, including Colonel Patton's regiment, which had also fought at Blue Mills Landing. When Patton arrived at Lexington, recalled I.V. Smith, a solider in his command, "the siege was in full blast, and we took part in it."[14]

On the nineteenth, General Harris, in his words, "directed a desultory fire to be kept up during the day by my sharp-shooters along my entire front," and at the same time, he ordered that rude field fortifications, consisting of ditches, logs, and other shelter, be constructed all along his line. In

Sketch of the Battle of Lexington. *From* Harper's Weekly.

surveying the hospital position in the afternoon, Harris hit on the idea of using hemp bales to extend the line of defense on both sides of the building, and he procured over 130 bales from General Price. Before being rolled into position, the bales were submerged in the river so they would not be set ablaze by the enemy's hot shot. Colonel Hughes, whose regiment helped defend the hospital position, reported, "These portable hemp bales were extended like wings of a partridge net, so as to cover and protect several hundred men at a time, and a most terrible, galling and deadly fire was kept up from them upon the works of the enemy by my men."[15]

The question of who came up with the idea of using the hemp bales at Lexington was a matter of some debate in the years after the war. Although Harris was often credited with the idea, other State Guard officers also claimed credit. In fact, the author of the 1881 *History of Lafayette County* devoted three full pages to a discussion of which State Guard officer actually deserved the credit. At least one veteran of the battle, a soldier in Harris's command, said after the war that the enlisted men started using the hemp bales on their own and that no officer deserved credit for the idea.[16]

The question of where the hemp bales came from is also a matter of some uncertainty. Sometime on the nineteenth, according to Captain Wilson, a wagon master named Thomas Hinkle hauled a large number of hemp bales from Wellington and dumped them on the streets of Lexington south and southwest of the Federal fortifications. These might have been some of the bales, mentioned by Captain Wyatt in his diary, that had been delivered to the State Guard camp on the seventeenth, and they might have been some of the ones Harris requisitioned from Price later on the nineteenth. Most sources state that the hemp bales came mainly from warehouses along the river, but even these sources sometimes disagree on which warehouses. It seems reasonable, therefore, to conclude that the hemp was probably retrieved from more than one location.[17]

While Price was receiving reinforcements and maneuvering his men into strategic positions, Mulligan was expecting reinforcements as well. He and his officers had told their men that, if they could hold out until the nineteenth, they would be reinforced, and according to Mulligan, "All through the day the men watched anxiously for the appearance of a friendly flag under which aid was to reach them, and listened eagerly for the sound of friendly cannon. But they looked and listened in vain."[18]

With Price surrounding the Union forces at Lexington, on the verge of breaking the Federal hold on the Missouri River, and threatening to take possession of the entire western half of the state, General Fremont tarried at St. Louis, blithely assuming that his orders to relieve Mulligan were being carried out. Not only was General Sturgis not "commanding at Lexington," as Fremont wrote on the eighteenth, but he had turned back and was heading the other direction. Colonel Smith and Colonel Scott had likewise turned back and were marching toward St. Joseph. Colonel Davis was still lolling at Jefferson City, complaining about the lack of necessary supplies to undertake a movement against Price. General Lane, who was supposed to be marching toward Lexington from the south, had his sights set, instead, on plundering Osceola.[19]

At least one of the Union's feeble attempts to relieve Mulligan turned into a complete fiasco. Four Indiana regiments were dispatched from Jefferson City to Lexington aboard steamboats on the eighteenth. On the evening of the nineteenth, as they approached Glasgow, they got word that a strong Rebel force occupied the place. Disembarking, the commanding officers sent out scouting parties in two different directions, and the two detachments, mistaking each other for the enemy, opened fire in a cornfield, killing twelve men. One of the Indiana soldiers not immediately involved in the incident called it "shameful and ridiculous." Retrieving their dead and wounded, the Union troops got back on their boats, and two of the regiments returned to Jefferson City in humiliation. The rest of the Indiana troops continued up the river, but beyond Cambridge, they "vanished from mortal eye," according to one critic. "Perhaps they are threshing new corn-fields in search of rebels, which is a good thing to do—if Col. Mulligan can wait."[20]

The longer Mulligan went without reinforcements, of course, the more precarious his position became. Not only was the State Guard net tightening around him, but also, and perhaps worse, he was running low on food and water. Lieutenant McClure recorded on the morning of the nineteenth that he'd had no dinner the day before but had finally gotten a "slap jack cake," made from flour fried in grease, at 10:00 p.m. "If we only had some of the crackers the men used to despise," McClure pined, "they would be a great treat."[21]

More pressing than the scarcity of food at the college fort was the lack of water. The weather had been unusually warm, and by the nineteenth, the water in the cisterns was used up. With the Union fortifications now cut off from the river, the water supply could not be replenished. The thirst of some of the soldiers became so desperate that they reportedly resorted to drinking vinegar. When a shower came up, others spread their blankets out in the rain until they were soaked and then wrung the water from them into their camp dishes. The respite from the "hot and dusty" weather, as Lieutenant McClure called it, proved brief, however. All day long on the nineteenth, according to Mulligan, his men "fought without water, their parched lips cracking, their tongues swollen, and the blood running down their chins when they bit their cartridges, and the saltpeter entered their cracked and blistered lips, but not a word of murmuring."[22]

During the late afternoon of the nineteenth, General Harris realized that soaking the four- to five-hundred-pound hemp bales in the river before rolling them into position as moveable breastworks was not such a good idea. "The wetting," he reported, "so materially increased the weight as to prevent our men in their exhausted condition from rolling them to the crest of the hill." He then adopted the idea of rolling the bales into position first and then wetting them so as to reduce the arduousness of the task.[23]

Before the new tactic could be fully implemented, a truce was called about 5:00 p.m. to allow the sick and wounded Union soldiers to be removed from the Anderson house and taken to a hotel in town, where they were ministered to by the ladies of Lexington. Robert Armstrong, one of the Union men moved to the hotel, remembered that many of the women—"the wives, mothers, daughters and sisters of the enemy—brought soap and clothing and washed our wounds."[24]

The evening truce of September 19 was renewed or extended at 8:00 p.m. to bury the dead and to allow the Union sick and wounded inside the fortifications, like those at the Anderson house, to be taken into Lexington. They were treated at various businesses and residences, including Dr. Cooley's home on Franklin Street, where the higher-ranking Union officers were housed. The terms of the truce, according to General Parsons, specified that the Union surgeons treating their sick and wounded in town would not be considered prisoners of war.[25]

During the truce, Mulligan received a message from Price demanding a surrender. Price proposed that the Federals would be allowed to leave unmolested if they surrendered, but if they refused, he would, in Mulligan's words, "hoist the black flag and show no quarter." Despite the worsening conditions inside the fortifications and despite the fact that some of his subordinates favored capitulation, Mulligan flatly refused the proposal, sending word back "that it would be time to settle that question when we asked for quarter."[26]

Not all of Price's subordinate officers agreed with him either. Some of them urged an all-out assault on the Union fortifications, but Price refused to put his men in harm's way needlessly and stuck to his strategy of patience. He reportedly said that there was no use killing the boys now when some of them would be killed soon enough anyway.[27]

The dire situation inside the Union fortifications was exacerbated by factors in addition to lack of food and water. Mulligan was also running low on ammunition, and many of his men were forced to pull double duty in order to guard the extensive fortifications. At the same time, he had too many men and animals that had contributed to the lack of food and water but were unable to contribute to resolving the predicament the Federals found themselves in. Armed with useless sabers and ineffective pistols, the Illinois cavalry could fight only after another soldier was killed or wounded so badly he could not use his weapon, and their horses were even greater liabilities. Many of the animals had been killed by stray shots, and the odor of their carcasses grew nauseating. "The suffering of the live horses and the stench of the dead ones were unendurable," recalled one Union soldier after the war. The bodies of dead soldiers left on the ground had also begun to stink, and they were given hasty burials inside the works during the evening truce.[28]

Some of the braver or thirstier Union soldiers ventured out during the truce to fill their canteens with water, and one detail even managed to bring back what Lieutenant McClure called "a barrel of brackish, muddy water," which, according to him, was all the water that was available to the Federals inside the fortifications. McClure said they would have had more except that the State Guard artillery broke the truce and fired two rounds of grapeshot at some of the men who were attempting to retrieve water.[29]

On the night of the nineteenth, Mulligan finally ordered two wells dug, and at least one of them was begun. When the effort turned up no water, however, the hole was filled with dead horses and covered back up.[30]

While Dr. Winer was allowed to return to the fortifications during the day on the nineteenth, Dr. Cooley was held in town to treat the wounded of both sides there. During the evening truce, he was permitted under parole to return to the Federal fortifications on an errand. As he passed the Federal line, he whispered to Captain Neet that he should expect a charge that night.[31]

The Federals with whom newspaperman Franc Wilkie had been traveling kept retreating northward on the evening of the nineteenth, but Wilkie, willing to run any risk to get a good story, decided to leave his escort and proceed to Lexington with or without General Sturgis. Accompanied by a couple local men who had volunteered to guide him, Wilkie reached Lexington late in the evening and was conducted to the building where General Price had his headquarters. Leaving Wilkie on the sidewalk, one of the men went inside to secure an interview for the reporter. Returning, the man led him upstairs to where a gray-haired gentleman was seated, and the escort surprised Wilkie by announcing, "Gen. Price, this is my *prisoner*." The reporter explained who he was and his purpose in coming to Lexington, but

Drawing of the Battle of Lexington based on a sketch drawn by newspaperman Franc Wilkie while he was held prisoner in the Missouri State Guard camp. *From* Frank Leslie's Illustrated Newspaper.

Price nonetheless turned him over to Provost Marshal Phineas Savery, who locked him as a prisoner in a nearby room, from where Wilkie was able to view part of the ongoing siege through a window.[32]

When the truce ended late on the night of the nineteenth, Guibor's battery, in the words of General Parsons, immediately "opened upon the enemy's fortifications." Coordinating with Colonel Rives, General Harris had used the lull in action to finalize arrangements for defense of the Anderson house position, and Colonel Rives's forces now began slowly rolling the hemp bales up the hills, gradually advancing behind them. At one point, some of Rives's men mounted a charge toward the Federal fortifications, but forewarned by Dr. Cooley, the Federals had stretched a picket rope in front of their breastworks, which tripped up some of the attackers and aided the defenders in easily repulsing the attack.[33]

Lieutenant McClure's accusation that the State Guard artillery opened up on some of the Union soldiers who sallied out to fetch water during the truce is unconfirmed by other sources, but it is certain that the Missourians closely guarded the springs outside the fortifications throughout the siege. On the late evening of the nineteenth, for instance, Colonel Hughes's infantrymen advanced behind their portable breastworks to within close range of the Federal fortifications, and during the night they killed as many as thirty Union soldiers, according to Hughes, and captured several others who were attempting to retrieve water from a spring and well on the grounds of the Anderson house. [34]

One Union soldier who survived a sortie outside the fortifications to fetch

Colonel John T. Hughes's State Guard regiment was stationed on the grounds of the Anderson house during much of the Battle of Lexington. *John T. Hughes, #30121, in the collection of Wilson's Creek National Battlefield. Courtesy of the National Park Service.*

water was Henry Carico, a soldier in Captain McNulta's Company A of the First Illinois Cavalry. At some point toward the end of the siege, although it's not clear exactly when, Carico made a mad dash to one of the springs to retrieve water for a dying comrade who was suffering as much from thirst as from his wounds, and the daring young soldier sprinted back through a hail of enemy lead using his finger to stop up a hole in his bucket made by a stray bullet.[35]

The State Guard might have intentionally or inadvertently fired on the Union water-seekers during the truce, but where the issue of retrieving water was concerned, the Federals, perhaps understandably in this case, didn't exactly abide by the so-called rules of war either. Colonel Bevier claimed that they often "took a little advantage of us" by sending out a woman to retrieve water from a spring near that part of the fortifications where his men were stationed: "She came and went repeatedly, and our noble Missourians, rough and uncouth as some of them were, although they indulged in good deal of profane language at her expense, fired not a single shot." A couple Union men who tried the same thing, on the other hand, were riddled with bullets before they had run ten feet.[36]

Lieutenant Barlow also recalled a woman sallying out from the fortifications to fetch water. On the morning of the nineteenth, she came out with several canteens and was allowed to fill them unmolested, but when she came back again later the same day with a bucket, "some of our old hunters, with their hair-trigger rifles," Barlow said, "had crawled up within a hundred yards and splintered the bucket in her hands. They could stand canteens from the fair sex, but drew the line at buckets."[37]

The previous two anecdotes involving women retrieving water were told years after the war, and they have the ring of romantic fancy. A more credible story might be the anecdote told by the author of the *History of Lafayette County*, who said that two women, the wives of officers, ventured out from the fortifications with buckets and were allowed to drink from the springs but had the buckets politely taken from them by some State Guard soldiers guarding the site.[38]

While conditions inside the Union fortifications were almost unbearable, the surrounding State Guard troops suffered their own privations. Although the days of the siege were warm, the nights turned cold, and most of the Missourians slept on the bare ground, many without blankets and some without coats. Two meals a day were delivered to them from the fairgrounds camp south of town, but few got enough to eat, and many were exhausted from lack of sleep.[39]

Their hardships paled, however, in comparison to those of the Federals lying inside their breastworks. Many of them had gotten nothing to eat and only a few sips of brackish water to drink on the nineteenth. As they lay down to try to sleep that night, the imminent threat of being bayoneted in the morning seemed hardly worse than the extreme hunger and thirst they were already enduring.[40]

Recalling the night of the nineteenth, one Federal solider said:

> *A horrid night followed a horrid day. There was no cessation of the firing. Musket shots interspersed with an occasional boom from a battery continued all night. We had neither eaten & drank for 24 hours. We subsisted on excitement. One place was as insecure as another. There was no rest. The scant luxury of a nap on the ground was out of the question, as the wail of the minnie [sic] bullet and the crash of the cannon balls against the college "murdered sleep."*[41]

Chapter 9

THE SIEGE OF LEXINGTON

Day Three

T he Missouri State Guard bombardment of the Federal fortifications
that resumed late Thursday night was kept up sporadically throughout
the wee hours of Friday morning, the twentieth. From the room where he
was confined on Main Street, Franc Wilkie could hear the roar of Old Sac, as
Bledsoe, who had rejoined his battery, fired hot shot at the Masonic College
in an apparent attempt to set the building on fire, but the newspaperman
surmised that the firing was meant, too, merely to harass the Union troops
by denying them sleep and keeping them on the alert.[1]

Friday morning dawned cold and damp, and the firing that had been
kept up at intervals throughout the night swelled to what Wilkie called a
"tremendous fury." Young Churchill Clark boasted that he would destroy
the college building, and both his and Bledsoe's batteries opened up on it
with new ferocity. Bledsoe's battery, in Susan McCausland's words, "tried
to tear up the earth. It thundered away so fiercely and continuously that
great holes were ripped in the walls of the college, and the already shattered
boarding house seemed likely to fall in a heap on its foundations." Meanwhile,
Mulligan's big guns answered only occasionally, either because ammunition
was getting scarce, as the county history stated, or because the Federals were
merely "lying low, waiting for a better opportunity to return their fire," as
Lieutenant McClure explained. One Union newspaper report claimed,
however, that the Union artillery answered "as soon as daylight revealed
localities sufficient to afford an aim," that the firing became so terrific on
both sides that nothing could be heard but the roar of guns and the rattle

of musketry, and that smoke enveloped the battlefield to the point that the combatants could not see one another.[2]

When the Federal artillerists did reply, their aim was often indiscriminate. One ball knocked a hole in a column of the county courthouse on Main Street, and several businesses and houses along the same street were also struck by cannonballs.[3]

Not long after sunrise, Rives's division on the grounds of the Anderson house and Harris's and McBride's divisions north and northwest of the college resumed the work they'd begun the day before of rolling portable breastworks, in the form of hemp bales, up the steep hills toward the Federal entrenchments. "Two or three men would get behind a bale," explained Captain Wilson, "roll it awhile, then stop and shoot awhile. A line would be advanced in this way as close as was thought proper, and while the men lay behind and fired, a second line would be rolled up and placed on top of the first."[4]

Another State Guard veteran recalled after the war, "It was a great spectacle to see that line of hemp bales moving slowly up the steep bluff and sharp shooters firing all the time." A contemporaneous newspaper report, on the other hand, described the scene from the perspective of the Union soldiers in much more vivid detail:

> The rebels presented a strong breastwork of hemp bales which appeared like a moving barrier, impenitrable to bullets or cannon shot and swarming with men in the rear. It was about twenty rods in length and the height of two bales of hemp. The bales were placed with the ends facing our fortifications, affording a thickness of about six feet. This immense breastwork commenced moving forward—not by detachments or singly, but in one vast body, unbroken and steady as though it slid along the ground of its own volition. It advanced steadily over the smooth surface, parting to pass trees and closing up again as impenitrable as a rock. Behind it were hundreds of men pushing and urging with levers, while others held the bales steadily to their places, and others still whose numbers were almost indefinite firing between the crevices and over the top, at our soldiers. Our men looked at the moving monster in astonishment. It lay like a large serpent, winding over the hills and hollows, apparently motionless, yet moving broadside on, to envelop and destroy them in its vast folds. In vain the cannon were turned upon it. The heavy bales absorbed the shot harmlessly, or quietly resumed the position from which they were displaced, seemingly moving without hands, but in reality controlled by strong arms which were unseen. In vain the musket balls rained upon it in unremitting showers. The thousands that

it concealed were safe from such puny assaults, and, slowly gliding along, they waited with eagerness the time when their position should warrant them in bursting through its walls and storming up to the intrenchments. Our brave soldiers could only watch it with keen anxiety, and wait for the fearful result.[5]

About 8:00 a.m. on the twentieth, General Price sent Kelly's battery back to support McBride northwest of the college fort. McBride was busy erecting a breastwork of hemp about one hundred yards north or northwest of the outlying lunette, where the Federals had planted an artillery piece since abandoning the position on the evening of the eighteenth. Meanwhile, to the left of McBride's position, General Harris's men were gradually advancing behind their moveable breastworks up the east side of the northwest promontory of College Hill toward the same lunette. As the two commands were engaged in this work, "a galling fire was kept up on both sides," according to General McBride. While allowing that "some of Gen. Harris' men and some of ours were killed and wounded," McBride was sure also that "the enemy suffered severely." General Harris, for his part, said that the steady, inexorable approach of the hemp bales "elicited the obstinate resentment of the enemy, who was profuse in the bestowal of round

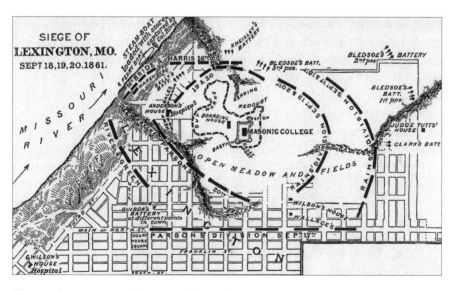

Nineteenth-century map showing the Union fortifications and the positions of the various State Guard forces surrounding the grounds. This map is generally accurate except that Colonel Green, at least during the crucial part of the fighting, was north of the grounds, not west of them as shown here. *From* Battles and Leaders of the Civil War.

and grape shot, and was not at all economical of his minie [*sic*] balls." The newfound stubbornness of the Federals suggested to McBride that Mulligan had only on this morning finally realized the strategic importance that the State Guard attached to the position surrounding the lunette.[6]

Brought up and planted behind McBride's breastwork of hemp, Kelly's battery opened fire shortly after nine o'clock. About the same time or shortly afterward, Harris's men rose up from behind their hemp bales and made a charge up the hill from the east toward the fortifications. The Missourians broke through the Federal line of entrenchments at one point, prompting even Lieutenant McClure to admire the "splendid charge" of the enemy. McClure said the fight was "awful," but the defenders, led by Captains James Fitzgerald and Patrick McDermott of the Irish Brigade, soon repelled the attacking party and regained full possession of their entrenchments.[7]

Describing the State Guard charge in extravagant terms, the *Chicago Times* reported that "eight thousand men emerged from the forest and charged on a run." Advancing with loud yells, the Missourians got to within about fifty paces of the entrenchments before the Federals opened fire "like a flash of lightning. It was like an avalanche of fire sweeping through the tall prairie grass. The men went down column after column." Daring and determined, the State Guard soldiers struggled to their feet, according to the *Times*, and impetuously raced into the fray again, trampling their dead comrades under foot, only to be mowed down again by a second volley from the Federal rifles. Finally, after a third charge that was just as disastrous as the first two, the Missourians "broke up in disorder and retreated" and did not stop until they had "gained the refuge of the woods." The newspaperman's flowery language and his estimate of the number of State Guard troops involved in the charge suggest that this was a highly exaggerated account. It is unlikely that as many as eight thousand State Guard soldiers were ever actively engaged at the same time on the entire Lexington battlefield, let alone in one small area of it. The actual number of Harris's men who made the charge on the morning of the twentieth was probably no more than several hundred, and the casualties were not nearly as great as the *Times* account implied.[8]

At some point during or shortly after Harris's charge, Major Becker of the home guards raised a white flag. Captain Wilson of the State Guard, who lived in Lexington and presumably knew Becker after the war, said this action came after the fighting had died down and that the flag was meant only to signal a truce to allow the Federals, some of whom had surged out of their entrenchments to repel the charge, to bring in their wounded.

Sketch depicting a Union charge over the embankments at the Battle of Lexington. *From* Harper's Weekly.

However, most Union sources, including Mulligan's account of the battle, seem to suggest that Becker raised the flag as an act of surrender while the fighting was still raging, that the flag was immediately ordered down, and that the fighting quickly resumed.[9]

While Harris and McBride were contending for the northwest promontory of College Hill, Colonel Hughes and the rest of Rives's division were keeping up an intense fire on the westernmost entrenchments from the grounds of the Anderson house. "The rivalry and enthusiasm became irrepressible and the conflict exceedingly sharp," said Hughes. "Our gallant and brave boys picked off every Federal that attempted to show his head above the breastworks." A Union account of the same action said that the Federals "were receiving obstinate attacks from a body of several thousand rebels, who were ensconced behind the hill upon which the hospital stood."[10]

South of the college fort, General Parsons maneuvered his command to sustain the State Guard troops engaged in intense fighting on the opposite side of the fortifications. At Captain Guibor's suggestion, Parsons ordered Guibor's battery, supported by Captain Champion's infantry, down Cedar Street (i.e. Eleventh) to within about two hundred yards of the fortifications, where, in the general's words, Guibor "opened volleys of grape on the enemy's works with decided effect" and "brought his guns to bear upon" the

Federals contending with Harris and McBride. In an apparent reference to Guibor's guns, a *Chicago Times* newspaperman, writing about the action on the west side of the fortifications, said that one of the State Guard batteries "swept our works with terrible force."[11]

Parsons ordered Colonel McCulloch down Main Street to College Street and then up College Street to take possession of a brick building within eighty yards of the Federal works. According to Parsons, McCulloch, in reaching this position, braved "a heavy volley" from the Federals and also came under friendly fire from one of the State Guard's own batteries (probably Clark's), which mistook him for the enemy. Colonel Alexander's regiment and Colonel Dill's regiment under Major David Herndon Lindsay were then ordered to move up and support McCulloch.[12]

As the fight raged, Colonel Mulligan personally commanded the Federal troops stationed nearest the Anderson house. At the same time, said one Union newspaper, he dashed about throughout the entrenchments "encouraging and directing the men." Disdaining to "walk in the trenches, where safety was sure," Mulligan "trod the high ground in the rear, where bullets flew like hailstones, heedless of the entreaties of the soldiers, who followed his manly form with their wondering eyes, and sent up shouts of acclamation at his noble daring."[13]

After Harris's morning charge was repulsed, the State Guard troops continued closing in on the Federal entrenchments behind their moveable breastworks until they got to within about fifty or sixty yards by early afternoon. Some of the Missourians might have been even closer than this. T.A. Fagan of Harris's division recalled that he and his comrades got "close enough to have thrown our hats over the enemy's works." With the State Guard troops so near the Federal lines, the defenders were now forced to hunker down in their entrenchments, whereas they had previously been able to move with some freedom inside the fortifications.[14]

A soldier in Colonel Peabody's command called the "steady and fatal approach" of the hemp bales a "rebel 'anaconda,'" and the hempen boa continued to slither closer to the Federal fortifications throughout Friday morning and into the early afternoon. "The woods swarmed with men," said the *Chicago Times*, "and every hill teemed with riflemen, while the treetops were alive with sharpshooters, who picked off our men continuously." Still, claimed the *Times*, there was no decided advantage on either side at this stage of the conflict.[15]

Then, at about two o'clock in the afternoon, Harris's men launched another charge up the eastern slope of the northwest promontory of College

Eastern slope of the northwest promontory of College Hill, as it appears today. The Missouri State Guard's final charge came from this direction. *Photo by the author.*

Hill. A Union report claimed this assault involved fewer State Guard soldiers and was more easily repulsed than the one earlier in the day, but be that as it may, the Missourians succeeded in capturing an artillery piece at the lunette and driving the Federal forces detailed to protect it back to their main line of entrenchments. The retreating forces included one company of home guards, one company of the Irish Brigade, and a detachment of Colonel Marshall's cavalry. Upon reaching the corral inside the fortifications, the fleeing Federals rallied, and along with another company under Captain Fitzgerald sent by Colonel Mulligan to reinforce them, they returned to the attack and forced the State Guard soldiers to begin withdrawing. Marshall's cavalry was sent out in pursuit of the retiring Missourians, and the horsemen charged down the slope "at a tremendous pace," according to the Union report, and scattered the retreating Rebels without resistance. They also recaptured the cannon, which they brought back to the fortifications "amid cheers and cries of exultation."[16]

Private Palmer, who was among the cavalrymen who made the afternoon foray, painted a much bleaker picture of the incident than did the Union newspaper. Palmer considered the order to charge "perfectly absurd," since he and his comrades were armed only with horse pistols and sabers, but he nonetheless galloped out of the trenches with the rest of the attacking party not far from Lieutenant Samuel Douglas, who was leading the charge. "The head of the column had no sooner debouched than a terrific fire met it," Palmer recalled. "Douglas received a wound in the leg and went at once to the rear. Two men and several horses were shot, the column hesitated then became confused, and went back to cover; which I thought a very wise thing to do."[17]

An account written by a member of Harris's command just two days after the fact suggests that the Union cavalry charge might have been neither as irresolute as Palmer remembered nor as successful as the Union newspaper claimed. "Col. Marshall's cavalry, six hundred, made one grand charge at the breastworks," said the State Guard soldier. "Our rifles opened upon them first and many a plumed warrior fell from his charger—as they advanced the muskets opened and still they came 'terrible as an army with banners,' but when the shot guns loaded with buckshot opened, human endurance seemed at an end, they wavered and finally fled in confusion."[18]

Shortly after the retreat of the Illinois cavalry, Colonel White was ordered to the charge at the head of about two hundred men, including one or two companies of Shield Guards, which, like the Montgomery Guards, was a prewar Irish militia unit from Chicago. "With brave hurrahs they dashed down the slope toward the serried ranks of the enemy," said the *Chicago Times*. When they were within a short distance of the State Guard line, the Missourians opened fire with a "terrible volley," which told upon the Federals with "startling effect." The front line of the attackers went down, including "the gallant commander," Colonel White. The Shields tried to rally, but a second volley caused them to break and retreat to the entrenchments, leaving the seriously wounded Colonel White on the field.[19]

About 3:00 p.m., very soon after White's ill-fated charge, Major Becker again raised a white flag from that portion of the entrenchments assigned to the home guards. Lieutenant Lawrence Harris of the Irish Brigade ordered the flag taken down, and an Illinois cavalryman who was manning a six-pounder reportedly turned his gun on the flag and "blew it into atoms." He then threatened to sweep into eternity any man who dared hoist it again.[20]

A story related in the county history suggests that Becker might have raised the white flag because he had been told, after Colonel White fell gravely wounded, that he was now in command, since all the other high-ranking Union officers were out of combat. Mulligan had been wounded in the arm by grapeshot from Bledsoe's battery and also in the leg from a rifle ball. Colonel Marshall was injured with a wound to the chest. Both Colonel Peabody and Major Van Horn were wounded, and Colonel Grover had been mortally wounded the previous day. Upon being told that he was in charge, Becker reportedly said in his strong German accent, "Vell den, I shtops this tamm foolishness poorty gwick."[21]

Although the white flag was quickly ordered down, it stayed aloft long enough that both sides ceased fire to try to determine its meaning. Confusion and panic reigned inside the Union fortifications, as many of the Federal soldiers left the entrenchments and retreated to the inner earthworks. Meanwhile, some of the State Guard troops, not sure what the flag meant, crept even closer to the Union line behind their hempen breastworks.[22]

General Price sent an envoy to Mulligan under a flag of truce with a message asking what the ceasefire meant. Unaware that Becker had raised the white flag, Mulligan wrote on the back of the message, "General, I hardly know unless you have surrendered," and he had the note returned to Price, who immediately dispatched the envoy back to Mulligan, assuring him that such was not the case.[23]

About four o'clock, after an hour's truce, Colonel Mulligan ordered his men back to the trenches, and hostilities resumed. Although the menace of the hemp bales loomed even larger now and the outlook for the Federals was increasingly dire, most of them still had no thought of surrender. Lieutenant McClure's Company D (aka the Earl Rifles) was "called to the rally," and McClure and his comrades dashed across College Hill through a hail of bullets toward their assigned position in the entrenchments. Just as McClure reached his post, however, he heard someone yell, "Don't fire, cease firing, a flag of truce!" He looked up, and sure enough, he saw a white flag waving from an opposite part of the fortifications. Threatened by the encroaching State Guard troops of Colonel Green, the home guards had abandoned the trenches at the brow of the northwest hill and retreated toward the college building, refusing to fight longer, and Major Becker had raised yet another white flag.[24]

Word of the white flag was sent to Colonel Mulligan, who was still stationed in the western part of the fortifications, and he ordered the flag down and tried to rally his men. Realizing the dire circumstances facing them, however, Mulligan's captains prevailed on him to save his men, and after a hasty meeting with his officers in a second-floor room of the college building, he reluctantly agreed to negotiate a surrender. An official flag of truce was then hoisted opposite Colonel Rives's position near the Anderson house. Captain McDermott of the Irish Brigade came forward requesting to discuss terms, and Rives sent a runner to General Price relaying the news.[25]

Immediately after the official white flag waved, a number of Union soldiers stationed at the college spilled out of the building and leaped over

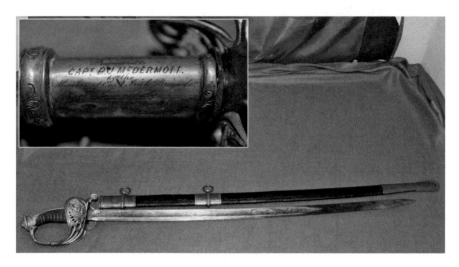

Sword and inscribed scabbard that belonged to Captain Patrick McDermott, who led a Union charge and later came forward to discuss terms on the last day of the battle. *Courtesy of Joe Maghe.*

the east side of the inner breastworks "like a lot of boys just dismissed from school," according to Colonel Snyder of Rains's command. Thinking the soldiers were mounting a charge on the State Guard line, Bledsoe, unable to see the white flag from his position, mistakenly fired two rounds at them before word of the ceasefire reached his battery. Fortunately, no one was hurt in the incident.[26]

Upon receiving Rives's message, Price sent Thomas Snead, his chief of staff, as an envoy to Mulligan to negotiate terms of a surrender. (Colonel Mulligan also sent an envoy, Major Charles Moore, to Price's headquarters.) Rives and his staff had already advanced to the Federal line, where they were greeted by Colonel Marshall and other Union officers, by the time Snead arrived. Snead and Marshall, acting as Mulligan's representative, then entered into negotiations. Marshall balked at the State Guard's demand for an unconditional surrender. Price's terms required the Union enlisted men to swear oaths not to take up arms against Missouri or the Confederacy and to give up their arms and equipment, retaining only their clothes and personal property. They would then be sent home. Price's intention to free the enlisted men on their oaths stemmed not so much from magnanimity as expediency because the State Guard did not have the means to guard and feed almost three thousand prisoners. The Federal officers, however, would be held as prisoners of war until an exchange could be arranged.[27]

Snead gave Marshall ten minutes to decide or else the State Guard forces would resume hostilities. Marshall left to consult with Mulligan, who reluctantly acceded to the unconditional surrender, and Marshall returned just as the ten minutes elapsed to inform Snead that the terms had been accepted. When news of the surrender spread among the Union soldiers inside the fortifications, "the scenes at the capitulation were extraordinary," according to the *Chicago Tribune.* "Col. Mulligan shed tears. The men threw themselves upon the ground, raved and stormed in well nigh frenzy, demanding to be led out again and 'finish the thing.'" Lieutenant McClure admitted that he, too, shed tears and "felt ashamed" of his weakness upon first learning that

Thomas L. Snead, as Price's emissary, negotiated the Union surrender. *Thomas Snead, #11352, in the collection of Wilson's Creek National Battlefield. Courtesy of the National Park Service.*

the Union forces had been compelled to surrender. Many horses belonging to the Illinois cavalry had already been killed during the siege, and when the surrender was announced, a good number more were reportedly killed on the spot by their owners, who were unwilling to let the animals fall into the hands of the victors.[28]

Meanwhile, shouts of celebration went up along the State Guard line when word of the surrender was received. "Hurrah! Lexington is ours! Once more She's free!! Hurrah for Jeff Davis & the Southern Confederacy! Such were a few of the wild huzzahs that rent the air," recalled one State Guard soldier. Another remembered, however, that the Missourians welcomed the surrender not so much because it meant victory but because they were hungry and tired.[29]

General Price came forward to personally receive the surrender of the Union officers in a roped-off area of the Anderson house lawn, while

General Parsons was sent inside the fortifications to receive the surrender of the enlisted men. Informed at first that he would have to give up his sword, Colonel Mulligan reportedly tried to break it in two. Seeing this, General Price told him he had fought bravely and it would be wrong to deprive him of his sword. All the other Union officers were also allowed to keep their swords.[30]

The State Guard troops soon surged forward to take possession of College Hill, many of them shouting hurrahs as they came. "The terms of surrender were scarcely agreed upon," wrote a Union correspondent, "ere the thousands that were lurking in the timber and behind the breastworks swarmed into the grounds and rent the air with their vivas of jubilation."[31]

After the surrender, according to Colonel Hughes, "Friendly greetings took place between Federals and Confederates who but a few moments before had been engaged in deadly conflict." Brothers Caldwell and Sam Dunlap spotted an uncle and three of their cousins among the Federal ranks, and Caldwell greeted them in a teasing manner, telling them "that they ought to have had better luck & not been caught in bad company." Sam was a little less charitable. "My sympathy for them did not reach out very far," he declared. "The color of their clothes (blue) did not suit me."[32]

Some of the victorious Missourians, of course, were even less friendly and forbearing than Sam Dunlap. When General Price spotted some of his state troops still gloating and celebrating their victory with boastful cheers after entering the fortifications, he reportedly turned to one of his generals and said, "There is not much to cheer for, order it stopped." Some of Price's other men, in passing by a group of Federals, supposedly pointed in triumph to hair tied to their hatbands that had been taken from the mane and tail of General Lyon's horse at Wilson's Creek.[33]

During the celebration, one of the Missourians scaled the college building, and "all eyes were turned to him," said Ephraim Anderson. "The stars and stripes were lowered, and our flag was raised over the pierced and shattered building, amid the shouts and cheers of the assembled thousands." According to another State Guard soldier, the Missourians planted both a Confederate flag and a blue state flag atop the college building. Some Union reports said the U.S. flag was dragged in the dirt and otherwise abused after it was taken down, although Lieutenant McClure recorded in his diary that it was handed to General Price. If so, Price or one of his officers probably kept possession of it.[34]

After the initial excitement attending the surrender subsided somewhat, the Missourians were put in formation to watch as Mulligan

Henry Carico, photographed with his company's tattered U.S. flag, which he carried away from Lexington. *Courtesy of the Abraham Lincoln Presidential Library and Museum.*

marched his men out to stack their arms and turn over their accoutrements. The Union soldiers were loath to give up certain items, particularly their company colors, and in a few instances, they managed to keep these items by secreting them inside their clothes or boots. For instance, Henry Carico, the young man who had dashed outside the fortifications to retrieve water for his dying comrade, wrapped the flag of Captain McNulta's company around his body and was able to carry it away. He and his fellow soldiers reportedly "seemed to reverence it with an almost idolatrous devotion" during their trip home, and Carico was photographed with it when he reached Illinois.

The small Confederate flag captured during the charge on the lunette on the evening of the eighteenth was another of the items the Federals were able to conceal. In addition, Price allowed Mulligan's men to keep their regimental flag, now torn and shredded, which had been presented to them by the ladies of Chicago.[35]

Price reported that he took 3,500 Federal prisoners (a slight overestimate), including approximately 125 officers. He also confiscated five six-pound artillery pieces, two mortars, over 3,000 infantry weapons, a large cache of ammunition, many sabers, about 750 horses, a lot of wagons and cavalry equipment, more than $100,000 worth of commissary supplies, and some other property. In addition, he regained most of the money, about $900,000, which Colonel Marshall had taken from the Farmers' Bank of Lexington, although about $15,000 in bank notes was missing. (Some of the missing funds were later found in possession of one Henry Bradburn, a soldier in Mulligan's regiment, who returned to Chicago and "held high carnival over the booty" before being arrested and returned to military authorities in St. Louis.) Price also recovered the great seal of the State of Missouri and the state records, which had been deposited at Lexington for safekeeping by Governor Jackson after he had been driven out of Jefferson City earlier in the year and which, Price said, "had been stolen from their proper custodian" by the Union forces.[36]

As the State Guard victory celebration continued, the grounds inside the Federal fortifications still told of the severe fighting that had raged for the past three days. "The scene in the college grounds was horrible," said State Guard soldier Eli McHenry. "Dead men, dead horses, the grounds and buildings torn to pieces, the sick and wounded in terrible plight." Ephraim Anderson recalled, too, that there were "trees riddled by balls, soldiers' apparel, blankets, knapsacks and canteens scattered about; guns, pistols, sabres and saddles were also lying around."[37]

Shortly after the surrender, the Union officers, accompanied by General Price, were marched from the fortifications and brought before another high-ranking State Guard officer, who was acting as the paroling officer. Refusing to take an oath not to aid or abet the Union army, the Federal officers were retained as prisoners of war but paroled into Lexington on their word of honor "not to 'run away,'" as Colonel Mulligan phrased it. They were housed at various spots throughout the town, including the City Hotel and the Virginia Hotel.[38]

After being marched into town, Lieutenant McClure recorded in his diary that the scene on what he called the "rebel battle-ground" was just as

Lafayette County Courthouse as it appears today, with an inset showing where a cannonball hit the top of one of the building's pillars. *Photo by the author.*

revolting as the view inside the fortifications: "It is a sickening sight—blood, brains, and fragments of limbs covering the ground profusely. The cellars where the dead and wounded lay look like slaughter-houses."[39]

With the permission of the sheriff, the State Guard took possession of the Lafayette County courthouse on Friday evening to use as a temporary storehouse for the arms, ammunition, and other spoils of war taken from the Federals. Colonel Snyder found some of Colonel Mulligan's private papers and returned them to him at the City Hotel, where he was staying as the prisoner/guest of General Price. Snyder, upon returning to the courthouse, found that the sentinels he'd left to guard it had done an admirable job of keeping unauthorized parties away, but still drunk with the heady spirit of victory, they had seized some of the most prized items for themselves.[40]

The Missourians' carnival of celebration spilled over into the streets of Lexington on the evening of the twentieth. One Union critic described the carousing in highly derogatory terms:

> *The scenes around the streets of Lexington Friday, after the surrender, beggar all description. The howls of joy and drunken jubilation coming from thirty thousand throats, made up a sound scarcely less than when, two*

days before, eighteen pieces of artillery and ten thousand small-arms were shattering the air in one hideous chorus. The officers of the Confederates were generally gentlemen, and behaved as such; but as for the common soldiers and their course that evening, I don't believe it could be equalled were all hell to be turned loose for a general carnival.

Whiskey, of course, was there—in men's brains, in their eyes, brandished in bottles, galloping "like mad" along the Street, hoarsely bellowing over the grand victory, cursing, blaspheming, yelling, babbling, hurrahing, lying in the gutter, insulting prisoners, quarrelling among friends—this and more did whiskey—the grand moving spirit that won the battle, and then rejoiced over its success.

...Scarcely a hundred of all the Confederate troops were uniformed; scarcely two had guns alike—no two exhibited the same trappings. Here went one fellow in a shirt of brilliant green, on his side an immense cavalry sabre, in his belt two navy revolvers and a bowie knife, and slung from his shoulder a Sharp's rifle. Right by his side was another, upon whose hip dangled a light medical sword, in his hand a double-barrelled shot-gun, in his boot an immense scythe, on his heel the inevitable spur—his whole appearance, from tattered boot, through which gazed audaciously his toes, indicating that the plunderings of many a different locality made up his whole. Generally the soldiers were armed with shot-guns or squirrel rifles; some had the old flint-lock muskets, a few had Minié guns, and others Sharp's or Maynard rifles, while all, to the poorest, had horses.[41]

The Union reporter's cynical view aside, the State Guard troops did have much to celebrate. As Captain James Tucker of Rains's division recorded in his company book after the battle was over, "This was indeed a grand victory for the South." More to the point, it was a great victory for the Missouri State Guard. General Price reported that the battle "demonstrated the fitness of our citizen soldiers for the tedious operations of a siege as well as for a dashing charge...No general ever commanded a braver or a better army. It is composed of the best blood and the bravest men of Missouri."[42]

In fact, the victory at Lexington represented the pinnacle of the Missouri State Guard. The Missourians, while still raw recruits, had won a minor victory at Carthage in July, and they had combined with Confederate and Arkansas troops to defeat General Lyon's army in August at Wilson's Creek. However, Lexington was their first significant victory fighting on their own. Spurned by McCulloch when he had proposed a combined march of State Guard and Confederate troops to north Missouri, General Price no doubt viewed the outcome at Lexington as sweet redemption. Even Captain Wyatt, the cynical State Guard surgeon who was wont to question Price's leadership, admitted that the general had done a good job at Lexington. Neither Price nor the men celebrating in the streets of Lexington on the evening of September 20, however, had any way of knowing that their first taste of victory as a fully organized army would also be their last.[43]

Chapter 10

THE SIEGE OF LEXINGTON

The Aftermath

O n Saturday morning, September 21, Isaac Hockaday, who lived south of town near where the skirmish on the morning of the twelfth had occurred, came into Lexington and visited the battlefield on and near College Hill, which, he said, "presented one scene of destruction. Horses Mules Men & Hogs lying in all directions, some dead whilst others maimed & mangled."[1]

Newspaperman Franc Wilkie was also permitted, under guard, to view the battleground on Saturday morning. Walking to the college grounds, Wilkie noticed a number of large brick buildings that had been "scarred, seamed and shattered by cannon and musket shot." Upon approaching the grounds, he saw that the college building itself had "scores of ungainly openings, torn through by the Confederate cannon." He added, "An immense crowd, not thousands, but tens of thousands of people, male and female, blocks the street and throngs all over the ground, peers from the college windows, jams the doorways and rambles curiously over the grounds."[2]

Once inside the grounds, the first thing Wilkie noticed was the "horrid odor of rotting flesh," and as soon as he reached the dormitory or boardinghouse northwest of the college, he realized where the stench was coming from:

> *In every direction lay horses, bloated to an enormous size, while in front of the building lay fourteen bodies of National soldiers in all hideousness of death and in all the noisomeness of far advanced decomposition. All lay upon the ground, a few with their faces covered and their hands folded*

reverently across their breasts; others displayed their stony motionless eyes, lips clotted with gore and ghastly countenances, surrounded by a dark, thick pool of blood that has welled from a bullet-hole in forehead or heart. In this building were some sixty or seventy wounded, dirty, bleeding, wretched, groaning in agony, covered with flies, dirt and filthiness and disgusting in every respect to the last degree.[3]

Going west toward the Anderson house, Wilkie discovered seven more bodies "with countenances black and putrid with decomposition," and "the worms had already commenced their work, and were crawling in thousands over cheek, lip and forehead." On the north side of the house were trees scarred by bullets, more dead horses and mules strewn about, broken wagons, shattered muskets, and other signs of a desperate battle.[4]

Wilkie then retreated to the college building and found that, among the three main buildings on College Hill, it "showed the most evidences of the skill of the Confederate artillerists. Through every wall and story, and through every room and hall had torn the iron hail, smashing, tearing and destroying, till the once noble edifice resembled an unsightly pile of brick."[5]

Father Butler, who was among the Union officers still being held, became a guest of Colonel Kelly of Parsons's division and celebrated Mass at Kelly's tent on the morning after the surrender. He visited sick and wounded Catholics on both sides without partiality and ministered to Catholics throughout the State Guard army.[6]

Many of the Missourians had retired to their camp at the fairgrounds after the celebration died down on Friday evening, but Price left enough men to guard the Union prisoners at the fortifications. On Saturday afternoon, the prisoners were put in formation and made to swear oaths not to take up arms against Missouri or the Confederacy until exchanged. A number of them objected strenuously to this, but all eventually complied except a few, like Private Palmer, who were able to slip out of the fortifications without taking the oath by pretending to be Southerners.[7]

The Union soldiers were compelled to listen to a harangue by Governor Jackson. The governor supposedly "addressed them in harsh language demanding what business they had to make war in the State of Missouri, adding that when Missouri needed troops from Illinois, she would ask for them." Price also briefly addressed the Illinois soldiers, telling them that they had fought bravely.[8]

The men of the Irish Brigade and the First Illinois Cavalry were then marched out of the fortifications to the strains of "Dixie" played by the

Sketch depicting Governor Jackson's harangue to the captured Union soldiers. *From*
Harper's Weekly.

State Guard bands. Their march was also accompanied by the taunts of
bystanders and what the *St. Louis Missouri Republican* called "the liberal
curses of the Confederate troops who lined the streets." General Price soon
put a stop to the jeering, proclaiming that the Union soldiers were not be
disturbed. The Federal soldiers were put across the Missouri River and,
according to the *Missouri Republican* and a few other Union sources, turned
adrift without food and water to make their way home on their own. This
accusation was apparently not true, however, as other sources, including
some Union ones, state that the Illinois troops were taken across the river
and marched to Richmond under the escort of General Rains, who treated
them very well. At one point, Rains appropriated a whole flock of sheep for
the Union soldiers, and the residents along the way also gave them provisions
and treated them humanely.[9]

The next day, September 22, Peabody's Thirteenth Missouri Infantry
and the home guards were turned loose on parole, as the Illinois troops had
been the day before. The local members of the home guard simply walked
to their residences in and around Lexington and were greeting family
members within minutes after their release. General Price is reported to
have personally turned some of them over to their wives "to be kept out of
future mischief."[10]

Union newspapers tried to put the best face possible on the Federal setback at Lexington, mainly by overstating Price's losses. Some of the Union estimates of Missouri State Guard losses were even more extravagant than their estimates of Price's total strength had been. One account, for instance, suggested that Price lost 100 killed and 300 to 400 wounded in the skirmishing on September 12 alone. Another report estimated the total State Guard losses during the entire siege at 3,000 to 4,000 killed and about the same number wounded. Although not as exaggerated as some of the newspaper accounts, General Fremont's report to the secretary of war placed the number of enemy killed and wounded at 1,400. General Price, on the other hand, gave his losses as 25 killed and 72 wounded. A study of the after-action reports of the individual State Guard commanders suggests that this was an underestimate but not nearly as far off the mark as the overstated Union calculations. The actual loss of the Missourians was probably at least 30 killed and 120 wounded, not counting any casualties that might have occurred among civilians like the old Texan who fought during the day and went home to supper every night.[11]

After General Price's after-action report was released, some Union observers took issue with his low casualty count. Upon his return to Chicago in mid-October, for instance, Father Butler pointed out that Price's estimate did not include the casualties among combatants who were not officially enrolled in his army, and Butler estimated that these losses were just as great as those among the officially enrolled soldiers. In addition, he insisted that Price had far underestimated the loss among his officially enrolled soldiers. By way of illustration, Butler claimed that he had personally helped bury seventeen dead Missourians whom Price had left on the field after the September 12 skirmish.[12]

On the other hand, by late September, even some Union sources grudgingly began to admit that the initial estimates of Price's losses were highly exaggerated. So even if Father Butler's statement about helping to bury seventeen Missourians on September 12 were true, and even if Price did understate his overall losses, his estimate was still closer to the actual figure than some of the early Federal guesses.[13]

Although Union sources grossly overestimated the State Guard losses, their reports of their own casualties were fairly accurate. After consulting the muster rolls of the Federal forces engaged at Lexington, newspaperman Wilkie, in a report to the *New York Times*, enumerated all the casualties, listing them by name whenever possible. He placed the Union loss at about 36 killed, 117 wounded, and 8 missing, and other Union reports, including

Fremont's, were generally consistent with this estimate. The actual losses, however, might have been slightly more than Wilkie's estimate, since the casualties of the home guard, with the exception of Colonel White, were not included in his report.[14]

Besides exaggerating Price's losses, the newspapers also tried to rationalize the defeat by saying that it was due almost entirely to the privations suffered by the Federal troops. Citing thirst as the main culprit, the *St. Louis Daily Missouri Republican*, for instance, said, "Exhausted nature did what gun and sword had failed to do." There was, of course, considerable truth to this contention, but even some of the Union troops later admitted that they were not as parched as reported.[15]

In addition, the Union sought scapegoats on which to place the blame for the defeat at Lexington. Major Becker, in particular, came under intense criticism. Colonel Mulligan called Becker a "lily-livered man," and Lieutenant McClure wrote in his diary of the dishonor that attached to Becker because of his action in raising the white flag. The press reflected the same view, and in some cases the censure of Becker extended to the home guard as a group. A report in the *Daily Missouri Republican*, for instance, claimed, "The Home Guards, as a general thing, sneaked into the trenches and refused to fight

Abraham Lincoln ordered General Fremont to "repair the disaster at Lexington without loss of time." *Courtesy of the Library of Congress.*

at all." Only after the war did a few observers point out that Becker had probably done the sensible thing and saved many of his fellow soldiers from being uselessly killed.[16]

The home guards weren't the only Union soldiers to come under attack after the surrender. Referring to the "abject cowardice" of Colonel Marshall, the *Chicago Times* reported that not once did he pretend to lead his men but instead was kept constantly busy looking after his own safety and that he was often seen "skulking through the trenches" on his hands and knees. Years after the war, George Palmer recalled that, one time during the battle, he saw Marshall down on his hands and knees urinating, afraid to stand up. About two weeks after the surrender, Colonel Marshall wrote to the *St. Louis Missouri Democrat* defending his behavior during the battle, and several of his subordinate officers attested that his actions were no less brave than those of any other man.[17]

General Fremont also came under fire for not reinforcing Mulligan in a timely fashion. After wiring Washington, D.C., on September 23 to report the fall of Lexington and to say that he was personally going to take the field, Fremont received a message later the same day from Union general in chief Winfield Scott informing him that President Lincoln expected him "to repair the disaster at Lexington without loss of time." While the *St. Louis Evening News* was suppressed for criticizing Fremont, the other St. Louis newspapers rose to his defense, but out-of-state critics like the *New York Times* pointed out, "When a general in the field needs excuses, his case is lost." Congressman Blair had already been at odds with Fremont for a number of reasons, including the general's failure to reinforce Lyon at Wilson's Creek, and the defeat at Lexington gave Blair yet another argument to use in his campaign for Fremont's removal as commander of the Western Department.[18]

The press's effusive praise of Colonel Mulligan and the Irish Brigade was a subtler form of justification than the scapegoating of Becker, Marshall, and Fremont. The Federals might have lost the battle, so the argument went, but they didn't go down without a hard fight against overwhelming odds. The *Daily Missouri Republican*, for example, lauded Mulligan as "brave and resolute" and proclaimed that the defeat at Lexington was a "glorious" failure. One critic dared to suggest that, while Mulligan had fought well, he had planned badly by not crossing his troops to the

Francis P. Blair Jr. influenced President Lincoln to remove General Fremont from command after the Union defeat at Lexington. *Courtesy of the Library of Congress.*

north side of the river when Price first approached, but such skeptical voices were very rare.[19]

The Union press not only largely overestimated the casualties of the Missouri State Guard at Lexington but also published inaccurate reports about certain other details of the battle. For instance, Colonel White was widely reported as either killed on the field or mortally wounded when, in fact, he lived for several years after the war.[20]

In the days following the battle, the State Guard forces remained at the fairgrounds just south of Lexington, and prospective recruits continued to pour into camp. One report in the wake of the battle placed the number of men in Price's camp at close to fifty thousand. While this was no doubt another bit of hyperbole, other sources confirm that the victory at Lexington did spur enlistment in the State Guard, or at least it spurred interest. Many of those who streamed into Price's camp in the days following the battle, however, were mere spectators, "curious to witness our military array," as Ephraim Anderson said, and many of the prospective recruits also had changes of heart about joining up. In addition, many soldiers who had been with Price at Carthage and Wilson's Creek took furloughs, and even some of those who had joined just prior to the Lexington battle turned around and went back home. "Those who did not care to face the perils of war longer," explained Sam Dunlap, "& wanted an excuse to return to their 'families' or 'Sweethearts,' almost imagined the war was over & the honors gained by the victory at Lexington was sufficient glory for them as a Soldier."[21]

After being taken across the Missouri River on the evening of September 21 and escorted to Richmond, the Illinois troops marched another thirty-five miles north to the Hannibal–St. Joseph Railroad and took trains to Quincy, Illinois, where they began arriving on the evening of the twenty-third. Five days later, they were moved to St. Louis, where most of them were mustered out of service on October 8.[22]

In late September, General Fremont began amassing a large army in central Missouri. Detached from other Southern forces by two hundred miles and running low on ammunition and supplies, Price was ill prepared to meet the threat; so upon learning of the concentration of Union forces to his east, he made arrangements to evacuate Lexington and march south. He further reduced his diminishing numbers by sending some of the more poorly armed recruits back home with the understanding that they could enlist later at a more opportune time. On September 26, he paroled all the Union officers with the exception of Mulligan until they could be exchanged, and he detailed Captain Champion to escort them to Jefferson City. The next day, Fremont took a train from St. Louis to Jefferson City to personally take charge of his troops in the field, and Captain Champion arrived with his prisoners at the general's headquarters on the thirtieth.[23]

Colonel Mulligan refused parole, and Price made plans for him to accompany the Missouri troops on their march south. Mrs. Mulligan, who had bided her time at Sedalia during the siege and rushed to her husband's side upon learning he had been taken prisoner, asked to go along as well. Price finally agreed, but only on the condition that she leave her baby in Lexington, and the child was left in the hands of Mrs. Sara Hunter, a Southern woman.[24]

On September 30, Governor Jackson, to help finance operations of his Missouri State Guard, appropriated from the Farmers' Bank of Lexington over $37,000 of the funds General Price had recently restored, and Price's exodus began the same day, the troops marching south out of town to the strains of "Dixie" and "Listen to the Mockingbird" played by a brass band. The march covered about twelve or fifteen miles the first day, and the troops went into camp near Greenton, where some of the hungrier among them helped themselves to a sweet potato patch.[25]

According to one estimate, the number of State Guard soldiers had already decreased from a peak of eighteen thousand during the siege to about eleven thousand when the retreat began. This number continued to dwindle through desertion and sickness during the march south until, according to the same source, Price had only about seven thousand able-bodied men when he crossed the Osage River a week and half later, about the same number with which he had left Springfield in August.[26]

On October 16, Major Frank J. White, commanding a special squadron of about 180 men called the Prairie Scouts and supplemented by a detachment of 70 home guards from Johnson County, dashed into Lexington and drove out the State Guard troops, including Captain Shelby, that Price had left to guard the wounded Union prisoners. Major White freed about 15 Union captives, including Colonels Grover and White, and took about 60 prisoners of his own. He also seized a quantity of arms, some supplies, and two ferry boats. The next day, he captured a steamboat and placed the liberated Union soldiers on it, bound for St. Louis, where Colonel Grover died two weeks later. With the displaced State Guard troops regrouping and threatening to mount an offensive, White paroled his prisoners and marched out of Lexington on the seventeenth to catch up with General Fremont, who had started south with his army in pursuit of Price.[27]

Price's certification of Major Van Horn's exchange and release from parole. *From Robert Van Horn Papers (KC 297), State Historical Society of Missouri, Kansas City.*

In late October, as Fremont approached Springfield and Price camped in the Neosho area, the two generals perfected an agreement for an exchange of prisoners. Under the agreement, dated October 26, 1861, most of the Union officers captured at Lexington, including Colonel Mulligan, were exchanged by name on a one-for-one basis for Missouri State Guard officers captured at Camp Jackson. Approximately 530 other officers and men not specifically named in the agreement were also exchanged at the same time. Mulligan returned to Chicago by way of St. Louis and then went on to Detroit, where he delivered a speech in November detailing his experience at Lexington.[28]

Colonels Mulligan, Peabody, and Marshall reorganized their regiments shortly afterward, and most of the Federal soldiers who had been exchanged reentered the Union army. Many of the Lexington parolees who had not been exchanged were also ordered back into service, under the premise that their oaths prohibited only their taking up arms against Missouri, since Price's army was not part of the Confederacy at the time. Later in the war, some of Peabody's men were captured at Shiloh, and upon being recognized, they were executed for having violated the terms of their paroles, which had specifically forbidden their taking up arms against either Missouri or the Confederacy. To resolve the issue, the Union army again mustered the Lexington parolees out of service. (Peabody was killed at Shiloh, and Mulligan was mortally wounded in Virginia in July 1864.)[29]

Meeting at Neosho on October 28, 1861, Governor Jackson's exiled state government passed an ordinance of secession, taking Missouri out of the Union. Whether a quorum of legislators was present and other questions of legality concerning the vote remain subjects of debate to this day. Nonetheless, the news was received with great fanfare among the state troops, and the Confederate government formally admitted Missouri to the Confederate States a month later. On December 3, Confederate president Jefferson Davis signed a resolution thanking General Price and his men for their "gallant and meritorious conduct" during the war, "especially for the skill, courage and fortitude by which they gained the brilliant achievement at Lexington, Mo."[30]

Ironically, though, Missouri's entry into the Confederacy signaled the demise of Price's Missouri State Guard and the virtual end of any serious threat to Union forces in the state. Price was promptly nominated a general in the Confederate army with the understanding that he should bring as many Missourians as possible into the Confederate service with him. About the same time, General Fremont was removed from his duties by President Lincoln, and the Federal forces withdrew from southwest Missouri. In late December, Price's state troops moved up and occupied Springfield, where Price set up a recruiting camp for the Confederacy. Some of his Missourians refused to enter Confederate service, but not enough to keep the State Guard from disintegrating over the next few months into a fragmented army that was reduced mostly to guerrilla activity and was never again an effective, organized fighting force.[31]

In early 1862, General Samuel R. Curtis drove Price out of Springfield into northwest Arkansas, where Price joined forces with General McCulloch and General Earl Van Dorn. In early March, Curtis defeated the combined Southern forces under Van Dorn's command at the Battle of Pea Ridge, effectively securing Missouri for the Union. In early 1863, General John S. Marmaduke made two brief forays into Missouri for the Confederacy, and Jo Shelby, now a colonel, raided all the way to the Missouri River in the fall of 1863 but was quickly chased back to Arkansas. In the fall of 1864, General Price himself mounted the most ambitious threat to regain Missouri for the South when he led a Confederate army of twelve thousand men into the state, taking dead aim at St. Louis, where the Union's departmental headquarters was located. Stalled at Pilot Knob before he could approach St. Louis, he crossed the state to the west, engaging in skirmishes with Federal forces along the way, including the so-called Second Battle of Lexington on October 19, 1864, which amounted only to some minor skirmishing between opposing pickets. Soundly defeated at the Battle of Westport on October 23, Price beat a hasty trail for Arkansas, suffering additional defeats at Mine Creek and Newtonia during the retreat. The Union in Missouri would not be seriously threatened again throughout the remainder of the war.[32]

Thus, the ground gained by the Missouri State Guard at the Battle of Lexington proved brief, and the glory was fleeting for the men who won the victory. In 1912, more than fifty years after the battle, Colonel Snyder offered a sober assessment of its significance that seems as apt today as it was then: "Our brilliant achievement at Lexington was barren of results, save to demonstrate the fact that the sentiment of Missouri was not in harmony with the secession movement. General Price...planned well, but the substantial Missourians were more interested in the conservation of their property and scalps, than in sacrificing anything for the defense of any mere abstract principle."[33]

Chapter 11

PRESERVATION AND COMMEMORATION

In the years immediately after the Civil War, most of the activity pertaining to the Battle of Lexington and the grounds on which it was fought was incidental rather than aimed specifically at commemorating the battle or preserving the grounds. At the close of the war, the Anderson house, which had remained in the hands of the Union army throughout the war, became the property of the Tilton Davis family. None of Oliver Anderson's original furniture survived the war, but the Davis family began restoring the building. Davis's appreciation of history prompted him not to repair many of the holes in the exterior walls that had been made by cannonballs during the battle, and these are still visible today. In 1868, ninety-one bodies of Union soldiers who had been given hasty, mass burials in trenches on the college grounds during or immediately after the Battle of Lexington were dug up and reinterred at Leavenworth, Kansas. The Masonic College building and grounds were used briefly after the war as a military school for boys but were donated by the Masons in 1871 to the Central Female College, later called the Central College for Women. In 1872, John McNulta, who had been a captain in the First Illinois Cavalry at the Battle of Lexington and was later promoted to brigadier general, conducted an inquiry for the U.S. Army into the controversial hospital episode on the first day of the siege. The findings of the inquiry essentially were that both sides had acted improperly but that both sides were also somewhat justified in their actions.[1]

One of the first events designed specifically to commemorate the Battle of Lexington was the Blue and Gray Reunion held in 1886, twenty-five years after the battle. Soldiers from both sides of the battle were invited to Lexington, and Mrs. Mulligan was invited to come from Chicago as the guest of honor. In the spirit of reconciliation the reunion was meant to foster, Mrs. Mulligan insisted that she would accept the invitation only on the condition that Sara Hunter, the Southern woman who had babysat the Mulligan baby in the days after the battle, be invited as a co–guest of honor. And so Mrs. Hunter traveled to Lexington from California, and together

Monument to the Confederate dead at Machpelah Cemetery. *Photo courtesy of John Maki.*

she and Mrs. Mulligan watched the parade of old veterans as they passed in review in front of them.[2]

Similar reunions were held during succeeding years, including one in September 1890, when survivors of the battle met in Lexington to determine the location of and the role played by the various units during the battle, to make a correct map of the battleground, and to gather historical information about the battle.[3]

In 1894, a Confederate monument was placed in Machpelah Cemetery by the Confederate Monument Association commemorating the Missouri State Guard soldiers killed at the Battle of Lexington, including a number who had been buried near where the monument was placed.[4]

On March 10, 1896, George H. Palmer, who had risen from a bugler and private in the First Illinois Cavalry to become a captain before the Civil War was over, was awarded the Medal of Honor for his bravery in leading the charge to retake the Anderson house hospital on September 18, 1861.[5]

The fancy sword that General Price had allowed Colonel Mulligan to keep on the day of his surrender mysteriously disappeared the next day. Many years later, about 1899 or 1900, a man walked into a lawyer's office in Lexington and turned over the sword, saying that he had stolen it the day after the battle when he was a but a lad and hid it on his farm not far from Lexington. After keeping it all those years, he wanted to clear his conscience, and the lawyer, who had previously corresponded with the Mulligan family, promptly sent the sword to Mrs. Mulligan in Chicago. A member of the Lexington Historical Society, however, wrote to the family shortly afterward suggesting that the sword might be donated to the society at some future time, and it was soon returned to Lexington, where it still rests at the Lexington Historical Museum.[6]

In 1903, the Lexington Historical Society published a book entitled *The Battle of Lexington*. It remains today a valuable resource for historians because it consolidates under one cover a number of after-action reports and narratives of the battle. These include the reports of twelve different Missouri State Guard officers, the text of Colonel Mulligan's Detroit speech, and two reminiscences written especially for the book, one by Major Van Horn and one by Captain Wilson.[7]

In the early 1900s, two bodies of Union soldiers were uncovered and reburied when work to extend the Central College for Women was going on. Then, in early October 1932, three more bodies were discovered in a burial trench when a road was being built through the Central College park. About a month later, on Armistice Day, all five unknown soldiers

Monument to the five unknown Union soldiers who were reburied in 1932. *Photo by the author.*

were reburied in a common grave on the battlefield during a ceremony attended by a large crowd. The carriage that bore the casket was escorted by members of the local American Legion, the Lexington chapter of the United Daughters of the Confederacy laid a wreath, and former Lafayette County prosecutor Isaac Newton Skelton III was a guest speaker. A granite marker was dedicated at the burial site, which is located just northwest of the present-day Lafayette County Regional Health Center. At the same time, a stone was also placed marking the spot where the bodies had been dug up. It is now located in the health center parking lot.[8]

In 1915, the Davis family moved out of the Anderson house, and it was purchased by some local citizens, who turned it over to the Central College for Women for preservation. However, the house was vacated in 1923, and it fell into disrepair and suffered at the hands of vandals over the next couple of years. In 1925, the college closed, and Lafayette County acquired the house. The county also took over the north part of the battlefield, which previously had been used as pastureland, and turned it and the Anderson house into a park and museum. Improvements, such as plaster repair and cleaning of woodwork, were made to the house in 1933–34 under a WPA program.[9]

In 1928, a monument was erected and dedicated on the campus of the Wentworth Military Academy marking the spot where Guibor's battery shelled the Masonic College on September 12, 1861.[10]

The old college building burned in 1932, and it was replaced by a one-third-scale replica on the same site. The replica and four columns marking the corners of the original building were dedicated in 1934.[11]

One-third replica of the Masonic College and posts showing the location of the corners of the original college. *Photo by the author.*

In 1955, the Anderson House and Lexington Battlefield Foundation was organized to preserve and promote the battlefield site, and the Lafayette County Court conveyed the entire property to the group. A reenactment of the Battle of Lexington was held the same year, and plans were formulated to develop the site as a tourist attraction. When the locally led effort stalled because of limited resources, foundation members met with Missouri State Park officials to discuss making the site a state park.[12]

On January 1, 1959, the property was conveyed to the state park board for restoration and development. Architect Kenneth E. Coombs was hired to conduct a study of the property and develop a master plan for the proposed restoration and development. After months of archival study and on-site research, he presented his report to the park board in January 1961.[13]

A centennial reenactment of the battle was held in May 1961 and attended by about twenty thousand spectators. It was staged by cadets from Wentworth Military Academy, assisted by other military and ROTC units. A parade was held in connection with the event, and Governor John Dalton attended as grand marshal. Later the same year, the Lafayette County Historical Society sponsored a commemoration of the Battle of Lexington on September 20, exactly one hundred years after the last day of the battle. In the days leading up to the event, *Lexington Advertiser-News* managing editor Bill Dye wrote a three-part series recounting the battle, and on the day of the event, Floyd C.

Monument to the Missouri State Guard erected by the Sons of Confederate Veterans near the visitors' center at the Battle of Lexington State Historic Site. *Photo by the author.*

Shoemaker, secretary emeritus of the State Historical Society of Missouri, was a guest speaker and laid wreaths at both the Confederate monument in Machpelah Cemetery and the Union monument on College Hill at the grave of the unknown soldiers.[14]

In September 2000, the Sons of Confederate Veterans dedicated a monument to the Missouri State Guard soldiers who fought at Lexington and placed it near the entrance to the historic site visitors' center. In September 2009, the Sons of Union Veterans placed a monument on the Lexington battlefield near the previous monument to the unknown

In memory of Colonel James Adelbert Mulligan and the members of his command who fought and died during the battle and siege of Lexington, Missouri, September 12-20, 1861. Colonel Mulligan commanded Union volunteers from Illinois and Missouri who fortified College Hill and stubbornly resisted the attacks of the Missouri State Guard forces of General Sterling Price. With their ammunition, water and rations depleted and reinforcements unable to reach them, Mulligan's forces were compelled to surrender.

May the people of the United States never forget the Union defenders of Lexington, who suffered and died that this nation might live forever free.

"they determined to do their duty at all hazards" Colonel James A. Mulligan

Erected in 2009 by the Department of Missouri, Sons of Union Veterans of the Civil War

Monument to the Union soldiers who fought at the Battle of Lexington erected on the battlefield by the Sons of Union Veterans. *Photo by the author.*

soldiers and dedicated it to all the Union soldiers who fought at the battle. Among the guest speakers at the latter event was U.S. congressman Ike Skelton, whose father had spoken at a similar ceremony seventy-seven years earlier.[15]

The Visitor Center at the Battle of Lexington State Historic Site. *Photo by the author.*

In 2011, the Missouri Department of Natural Resources' Division of State Parks and Big River Ranch sponsored a sesquicentennial reenactment and commemoration of the Battle of Lexington from September 16 to 18. Approximately eleven thousand people attended the event, and about one thousand members of the Missouri Civil War Reenactor Association participated in the reenactment on Sunday, September 18, at Big River Ranch just outside Lexington. Other events during the weekend included a parade through downtown Lexington, a Civil War film festival, tours of the Anderson House, and bus tours of Civil War sites throughout Lexington.[16]

Although the State of Missouri made strides toward developing the Lexington battlefield as a state historic site after it took over the property in 1959, for many years the only structure at the site other than the Anderson House was a small office where visitors checked in to tour the house. Development continued to lag until 1994, when a Visitor Center containing memorabilia and information about the battle, was completed. About twenty-eight thousand people now pass through the visitors' center each year. Places of interest throughout the battlefield are marked by informational signs, and self-guided walking tours are available. Motorists can also visit other points of interest throughout the town pertaining to the battle, such as Machpelah Cemetery. The Battle of Lexington State Historic Site park is open from sunrise to sundown year-round. However, office and visitors' center hours vary according to the season, and Anderson House tours are not offered during the winter except by appointment. Call 660-259-4654 or visit http://www.mostateparks.com/park/battle-lexington-state-historic-site for more information.[17]

NOTES

Works frequently cited are identified by the following abbreviations:

B&L: Johnson and Buell, *Battle and Leaders of the Civil War.*
CMS: *Columbia Missouri Statesman.*
CV: *Confederate Veteran.*
HofLC: *History of Lafayette County,* 1881.
LDH: *Louisiana (MO) Democratic Herald.*
LHS: Lexington Historical Society, *The Battle of Lexington,* 1903.
MHR: *Missouri Historical Review.*
NYT: *New York Times.*
OR: *The War of the Rebellion: A Compilation of the Official Records of the Union
    and Confederate Armies.* All citations refer to Series I unless otherwise stated.
SLDMR: St. Louis Daily Missouri Republican.

CHAPTER 1

1. *Oliver Anderson House*; Monaghan, *Civil War,* 185; *HofLC,* 273, 436–44.
2. McCausland, "Battle of Lexington," *MHR,* 127.
3. I consulted a variety general sources about the Civil War in Missouri. See
    especially Stevens, *Centennial History,* 701–47.
4. McCausland, "Battle of Lexington," *MHR,* 127; *HofLC,* 329.
5. McCausland, "Battle of Lexington," *MHR,* 128.

6. "Missouri History: Geographical Distribution of Slavery"; *HofLC*, 329.
7. *HofLC*, 330.
8. *HofLC*, 329; Haerle Family History. The county history incorrectly reported that this meeting occurred in mid-May.
9. Haerle Family History.
10. Ibid.
11. Ibid.
12. Ibid.
13. "May 10, 1861: The Capture of Camp Jackson in St. Louis."
14. McCausland, "Battle of Lexington," *MHR*, 127.
15. Stevens, *Centennial History*, 701–47; Snead, *Fight for Missouri*, 200.
16. *OR*, 3:11–12.
17. Ford, *Reminiscences*.
18. McGregor, *Rambling Reminiscences*, 1.
19. Lehr, *Mockingbird*, 16.
20. Anderson, *Memoirs*, 21.
21. *HofLC*, 332; *OR*, 3:101; Britton, *Civil War*, 24–29.
22. McCausland, "Battle of Lexington," *MHR*, 128.
23. *HofLC*, 332.
24. Ibid., 249, 434.
25. Ibid., 330, 368.
26. Snead, *Fight for Missouri*, 215–16.
27. Snead, *Fight for Missouri*, 216; *OR*, 3:11; *HofLC*, 334; McGregor, *Rambling Reminiscences*, 2.

Chapter 2

1. *OR*, 3:14.
2. Williams, "Role of German Immigrants"; *HofLC*, 335.
3. McCausland, "Battle of Lexington," *MHR*, 128–29.
4. U.S. census; McCausland, "Battle of Lexington," *MHR*, 129; *HofLC*, 335–36.
5. White, Papers, Memoir of Colonel Robert White and letter from R.M. Henderson to Colonel White, July 9, 1861.
6. Love, Letters, James Love to "My Dear Molly," July 14, 1861.
7. *HofLC*, 336, 364; *NYT*, July 21, 1861.
8. White, Papers, Letter to Colonel White, July 12, 1861.
9. *HofLC*, 336; U.S. census; *Past and Present of Rock Island County*, 198.

10. *HofLC*, 337; White, Papers, memoir.

11. *NYT*, July 21, 1861; White, Papers, memoir.

12. White, Papers, memoir.

13. Ibid.; *HofLC*, 336; Geiger, *Financial Fraud*, 90.

14. White, Papers, memoir; *Staunton (VA) Spectator*, September 3, 1861.

15. White, Papers, Shelby to White, July 30, 1861.

16. Ibid., Citizens to White, August 15, 1861, and memoir.

17. *HofLC*, 337; White, Papers, memoir. White identified the man left in charge at Lexington when Stifel's regiment returned to St. Louis as Fisher, but he almost certainly meant Becker and simply got the name wrong.

18. White, Papers, memoir; Love, Letters, James Love to "My Dear Molly," October 4, 1861; Brown, Narrative, 2.

19. *HofLC*, 338; McCausland, "Battle of Lexington," 130; *White Cloud Kansas Chief*, September 19, 1861. Mrs. McCausland mistakenly said the death of Withrow occurred during mid-September after Price reached Lexington; in fact, it occurred during the so-called First Siege of Lexington in late August.

20. *HofLC*, 338; Benton, "Autobiography"; *White Cloud Kansas Chief*, September 19, 1861; Brown, Narrative.

21. *HofLC*, 339; *White Cloud Kansas Chief*, September 19, 1861; *NYT*, September 13, 1861.

22. *NYT*, September 30, 1861; *HofLC*, 337; Dyer, *Compendium*, 1329; *SLDMR*, September 27, 1861.

23. *HofLC*, 337.

24. White, Papers, Shelby to White, September 1, 1861; *White Cloud Kansas Chief*, September 19, 1861.

25. *OR*, 3:165, 483; Moore, *Rebellion Record*, 77; *HofLC*, 338; Hewett, *Supplement*, 37:358.

26. *OR*, 3:165, 483; Moore, *Rebellion Record*, 72, 77; *HofLC*, 338; Grover, "Colonel Benjamin Whiteman Grover," 136.

CHAPTER 3

1. *OR*, 3:15–27; Burchett, *Battle of Carthage*, 173.

2. Castel, "Siege of Lexington," 4.

3. *OR*, 3:185; *OR*, 53:435–36.

4. Wyatt, "Confederate Diary," 8–9.

5. Ibid., 9.

6. Ibid., 9; Sitton, Memoir.

7. McDonald, "Capture of Lexington," 105; Sitton, Memoir; *OR* 3:185; *HofLC*, 339.
8. *OR*, 3:185. Price said in his report that he camped near Rose Hill on September 10, but other sources and the chronology of later events in his own report make it clear that he camped there on the ninth.
9. Luff, *Palmer Journal*, 4; LHS, 28; Moore, *Rebellion Record*, 73; Hewett, *Supplement*, 38:104; OR, 3:171.
10. *OR*, 3:186; Sitton, Memoir; Soldiers' Records; Anderson, *Memoirs*, 61; *HofLC*, 342.
11. *OR*, 3:186; Sitton, Memoir; Anderson, *Memoirs*, 62.
12. *B&L*, 308; Monaghan, *Civil War*, 187; Moore, *Rebellion Record*, 440; Taylor, Narrative.
13. *OR*, 3:186; Anderson, *Memoirs*, 62.

Chapter 4

1. LHS, 28; Hockaday, "Letters," 53; *Gazetteer of McClean County*, 104. I have made minor corrections in spelling and punctuation in the Hockaday quote, as I have in a few other quotes throughout the text where I felt that such corrections would facilitate the reader's understanding. A report in the *St. Louis Missouri Republican* claimed the skirmishing on the night of the eleventh constituted a "sharp and decisive action" with "considerable loss" to Price's forces and about four Federals killed. But this report evidently misidentified the fighting on the early morning of the twelfth as having occurred the previous the night.
2. *OR*, 3:186; Hockaday, "Letters," 53–54, *B&L*, 308.
3. Anderson, *Memoirs*, 63; Hewett, *Supplement*, 37:358, 38:105.
4. *OR*, 3:186; *B&L*, 308; *HofLC*, 342.
5. LHS, 10.
6. LHS, 55; *B&L*, 308; Hewett, *Supplement*, 37:48.
7. Thomas and Thomas, Letters.
8. LHS, 10–11, 42, 47; Hewett, *Supplement*, 37:48, 358; Thomas and Thomas, Letters.
9. LHS, 47; *Higginsville Advance*, June 4, 1909.
10. LHS, 46–47, 50, 55; Hewett, *Supplement*, 37:48, 358; *B&L*, 308.
11. *HofLC*, 358.
12. *HofLC*, 342; *CMS*, October 4, 1861, quoting the *St. Louis Daily Missouri Democrat*.
13. *OR*, 3:186; LHS, 11, 42. Rains's division was actually still going by its original designation, the Second Division, at Lexington. Only later would

it be redesignated the Eighth Division to correspond with the Eighth Military District that Rains commanded. However, I have chosen to call Rains's division the Eighth to avoid confusion with Harris's unit, which was also designated the Second Division.

14. *OR*, 3:186; LHS, 29, 42.
15. Taylor, Narrative.
16. LHS, 29.
17. Anderson, *Memoirs*, 65; Moore, *Rebellion Record*, 79.
18. Anderson, *Memoirs*, 65.
19. Hyde, "Dear Sister."
20. Patrick, "Remembering the Missouri Campaign," 45; LHS, 29.
21. OR, 3:186; LHS, 29; Snyder, "Capture of Lexington," 2–3.
22. *HofLC*, 342; Thomas and Thomas, Letters.
23. *HofLC*, 343.
24. *HofLC*, 343; Tilly, *Brilliant Success*, 28.
25. *HofLC*, 343; Anderson, *Memoirs*, 65.

CHAPTER 5

1. Moore, *Rebellion Record*, 79.
2. LHS, 29–30.
3. Musser, "War in Missouri," Part 3, 43.
4. Moore, *Rebellion Record*, 79.
5. LHS, 30; Moore, *Rebellion Record*, 79.
6. *CMS*, September 27, 1861; *NYT*, September 20, 1861; Moore, *Rebellion Record*, 72,75; Hyde, "Dear Mother"; Lane, *Recollections*, 18; *LDH*, October 10, 1861; *B&L*, 309. Mulligan estimated the total area of the fortifications at eighteen acres, while other contemporaneous sources estimated the area at from five to fifteen. Captain Joseph A. Wilson, an MSG veteran who provided information for an 1870 map of the Union fortifications, gave an estimate of the distance between the inner and outer earthworks that seems to suggest that Mulligan was fairly accurate.
7. *B&L*, 309; Moore, *Rebellion Record*, 72, 78; *HofLC*, 343; Maki, Interview.
8. LHS, 28, 30. Although Price said he took about 3,500 prisoners when Mulligan surrendered, and Thomas L. Snead, his former adjutant general, confirmed that figure after the war, their reckoning might have been influenced by the estimate that had already become current at the time. The known totals of the individual Union units present at Lexington

do not add up to a figure approaching 3,500. The battalion under Major M.P. Berry, which was attached to Peabody's regiment and is sometimes counted among the forces at Lexington, was not fully organized when Peabody was ordered to Lexington, and it was left at Kansas City to guard the garrison there, although some small portion of Berry's men might have accompanied Peabody.

9. LHS, 27, 30; *HofLC*, 364. Contemporaneous newspaper reports and other statements of the number of artillery pieces available to the Federals at Lexington vary from as few as five to as many as nine. The county history said Mulligan had seven six-pounders and two mortars, including three six-pounders in Adams's battery of the Irish Brigade. However, Price said in his after-action report that he captured five guns and two mortars, and Mulligan specifically said that the Irish Brigade had but one six-pounder.

10. Luff, *Palmer Journal*, 3; Patrick, "Battle of Lexington," 56.

11. Wyatt, "Confederate Diary," 10; Anderson, *Memoirs*, 66; *NYT*, September 22, 1861, quoting the *St. Louis Evening News*.

12. Anderson, *Memoirs*, 67–68; McCausland, "Battle of Lexington," *MHR*, 130; *CMS*, October 4, 1861, quoting the *St. Louis Democrat*.

13. Moore, *Rebellion Record*, 79; *HofLC*, 343–44; LHS, 7. The burning of the houses was afterward a matter of some controversy, particularly since at least one or two of them belonged to Union men.

14. Luff, *Palmer Journal*, 4.

15. Wyatt, "Confederate Diary," 10; McCausland, "Battle of Lexington," 130.

16. Moore, *Rebellion Record*, 80.

17. Ibid.

18. Ibid.

19. Grimes, *Confederate Mail Runner*, 23; Moore, *Rebellion Record*, 73.

20. *OR*, 3:171–73.

21. *NYT*, September 22, 1861, quoting *St. Louis Evening News*; *CMS*, September 20, 1861, quoting the *St. Louis Missouri Democrat*; *OR*, 3:171–74.

22. Hewett, *Supplement*, 37:359.

23. Moore, *Rebellion Record*, 80.

24. Anderson, 66.

25. Patrick, "Remembering," 45.

26. LHS, 30.

27. Luff, *Palmer Journal*, 4–6.

28. Moore, *Rebellion Record*, 80.

29. *LDH*, October 10, 1861; Anderson, *Memoirs*, 66. An anonymous correspondent of the *Democratic Herald*, a soldier in Harris's command,

stated positively that the command arrived on Monday evening, which was the sixteenth, and other sources seem to suggest the later arrival as well. If Harris, in fact, arrived on September 16, the rumor among Union soldiers of his arrival the evening before must have stemmed from the arrival of his advance.

30. LHS, 30; *CMS*, October 4, 1861; *LDH*, October 10, 1861.

31. LHS 14; *HofLC*, 345.

32. LHS 30; *HofLC*, 364.

33. Moore, *Rebellion Record*, 80.

34. Wyatt, "Confederate Diary," 10.

35. *OR*, 3:175–76.

36. Hyde, "Dear Sister."

37. Wyatt, "Confederate Diary," 10.

38. Tucker, Company Book.

39. Banasik, *Missouri in 1861*, 181–82; Moore, *Rebellion Record*, 142–43; *OR*, 3:176–77.

CHAPTER 6

1. Moore, *Rebellion Record*, 143; *HofLC*, 345; *Liberty (MO) Tribune*, September 27, 1861. Union reports estimated the State Guard strength at Blue Mills at 4,400, but it was probably scarcely more than half that. See especially the breakdown of numbers by unit that Colonel Saunders provided in his report of the action printed in the *Liberty Tribune*.

2. Moore, *Rebellion Record*, 143; Lehr, *Deep River*, 34.

3. Moore, *Rebellion Record*, 142.

4. Ibid., 142–43.

5. Ibid., 142; *Liberty Tribune*, September 20, 1861; Smith, Memoirs.

6. Moore, *Rebellion Record*, 142.

7. Ibid., 143.

8. *Liberty Tribune*, September 20, 27, 1861; Moore, *Rebellion Record*, 143–44. Atchison gave an estimate of sixty Federals killed and seventy wounded, but this seems exaggerated.

9. Moore, *Rebellion Record*, 143–44.

10. Lehr, *Deep River*, 36.

11. Snyder, "Capture of Lexington," 3; Moore, *Rebellion Record*, 80–81.

12. McCausland, "Battle of Lexington," *MHR*, 131.

13. *OR*, 3:186; Anderson, *Memoirs*, 69, Wyatt, "Confederate Diary," 10.

Chapter 7

1. Anderson *Memoirs*, 69; LHS, 11.
2. Moore, *Rebellion Record*, 81.
3. Anderson, *Memoirs*, 69.
4. LHS, 30.
5. Anderson, *Memoirs*, 69–70.
6. McCausland, "Battle of Lexington," *CV*, 225.
7. Patrick, "Remembering," 46; *Lexington Advertiser-News*, September 18, 1961.
8. McCausland, "Battle of Lexington," *MHR*, 131.
9. Ibid., 131–32.
10. Patrick, "Remembering," 46.
11. Ibid.
12. Anderson, *Memoirs*, 70; McCausland, "Battle of Lexington," *CV*, 225.
13. Moore, *Rebellion Record*, 81.
14. Patrick, "Remembering," 46.
15. LHS, 43
16. *OR*, 3:188–89.
17. Winter, "'Amidst Trials and Troubles,'" 1–2; *OR*, 3:189.
18. *OR*, 3:189.
19. LHS, 35; Carter, "Short Sketch," 4.
20. LHS, 35.
21. Ibid., 51, 56.
22. LHS, 51; *Lexington Sesquicentennial Commemorative Book*, 17.
23. LHS, 51; Patrick, "Remembering," 46–47.
24. LHS, 12, 51, 56; *Chicago Times*, September 27, 1861; Hyde, "Dear Mother."
25. LHS, 47, 56; Sitton, Memoir.
26. LHS, 47; *HofLC*, 347; Moore, *Rebellion Record*, 75; McNamara, "Historical Sketch"; *CMS*, October 4, 1861.
27. LHS, 35.
28. Ibid.
29. LHS, 35, 51, 56; Wyatt, "Confederate Diary," 10.
30. LHS, 36.
31. McCausland, "Battle of Lexington," *CV*, 225.
32. Ibid.
33. *Chicago Times*, September 23, 1861.
34. *HofLC*, 347.

35. Moore, *Rebellion Record*, 77.

36. Ibid., 75–76.

37. Moore, *Rebellion Record*, 75; LHS, 56–57.

38. LHS, 31.

39. Smith, "Mulligan and the Irish Brigade," 169; *Chicago Tribune*, September 28, 1861; LHS, 31.

40. *HofLC*, 351; LHS, 7–8; *Chicago Tribune*, September 28, 1861; *Gazetteer of McClean County*, 106.

41. LHS, 8, 31.

42. McCausland, "Battle of Lexington," *MHR*, 133.

43. Luff, *Palmer Journal*, 7.

44. Ibid.; Armstrong, "Other Side," 467.

45. Luff, *Palmer Journal*, 7–8.

46. Mansur, "Incident of the Battle," 496.

47. Ibid.

48. Armstrong, "Other Side," 467.

49. Ibid.

50. LHS, 31; Luff, *Palmer Journal*, 8; Moore, *Rebellion Record*, 73.

51. LHS, 4, 14; *HofLC*, 348–49.

52. LHS, 31–32.

53. Moore, *Rebellion Record*, 441.

54. Anderson, *Memoirs*, 71; LHS 36, 63;

55. *Chicago Times*, September 27, 1861; *LDH*, October 10, 1861; Andreas, *History of Chicago*, 192. Some sources say it was the Illinois cavalry, not the Irish Brigade, that charged the lunette on the evening of September 18, but this is probably an error of confusion caused by the fact that the Illinois cavalry did undertake a similar charge two days later. Some sources also suggest that it was Colonel Grover, not Mulligan, who led the charge, and Colonel Grover was, in fact, involved in the action, if not its leader.

56. LHS, 48.

57. *Chicago Times*, September 27, 1861; Moore, *Rebellion Record*, 81–82.

58. *OR*, 3:189; Vivian, *Down the Avenue*, 88.

59. Banasik, *Missouri in 1861*, 182–83.

60. McCausland, "Battle of Lexington," *CV*, 226.

CHAPTER 8

1. Moore, *Rebellion Record*, 76.
2. McCausland, "Battle of Lexington," *MHR*, 134; McCausland, "Battle of Lexington," *CV*, 225; *HofLC*, 353.
3. Moore, *Rebellion Record*, 81.
4. Ibid.
5. LHS, 52.
6. Snyder, "Capture of Lexington," 3–4; Gifford, *Lexington Battlefield Guide*, 25.
7. LHS, 8, 9, 68.
8. Patrick, "Remembering," 47.
9. *HofLC*, 362; LHS 42, 60; Banasik, *Missouri in 1861*, 184; Nixon, "Reminiscences," 420–21.
10. LHS, 12, 43.
11. LHS, 60; Bevier, *History*, 305.
12. LHS, 37, 61.
13. Lehr, *Deep River*, 36.
14. Smith, Memoirs.
15. LHS, 37, 52.
16. *HofLC*, 357–60; *St. Louis Globe-Democrat*, September 19, 1897.
17. LHS, 12.
18. Ibid., 32.
19. *OR*, 3:177–78, 196, 500.
20. *CMS*, September 27, 1861; *NYT*, September 26, 1861; *Chicago Tribune*, September 20, 1861; *OR*, 3:182; Keith, Journal.
21. Moore, *Rebellion Record*, 82.
22. LHS, 32; Moore, *Rebellion Record*, 73, 82; *NYT*, September 25, 1861; *HofLC*, 352.
23. *OR*, 3:191; Lehr, *Deep River*, 38.
24. LHS, 38; Armstrong, "Other Side," 467.
25. Tilly, *Brilliant Success*, 39; LHS, 32, 43–44.
26. LHS, 31; Moore, *Rebellion Record*, 82; Banasik, *Missouri in 1861*, 185.
27. *HofLC*, 354.
28. *HofLC*, 352; Morton, "Early War Days," 156.
29. Moore, *Rebellion Record*, 76, 82.
30. *HofLC*, 343.
31. Ibid., 353.
32. Banasik, *Missouri in 1861*, 184–85.

33. LHS, 38, 44, 57; *HofLC*, 353. That Rives attacked the Union fortifications shortly after Dr. Cooley warned the Federals of such an attack is contradicted by Captain Wilson, who said that the Missourians, learning of the additional precautions taken by the Federals, made no assault.
34. LHS, 52–53.
35. Prince, *Transactions*, 511.
36. Bevier, *History*, 306.
37. Patrick, "Remembering," 47.
38. *HofLC*, 352.
39. Hyde, "Dear Mother,"
40. Moore, *Rebellion Record*, 82.
41. Taylor, Narrative.

Chapter 9

1. Banasik, *Missouri in 1861*, 185.
2. Ibid.; *HofLC*, 354; Moore, *Rebellion Record*, 82; McCausland, "Battle of Lexington," *CV*, 226; *CMS*, September 27, 1861; *Chicago Times*, September 27, 1861.
3. *HofLC*, 354.
4. LHS, 13.
5. Smith, Memoirs; *Chicago Times*, September 27, 1861.
6. LHS, 38, 48.
7. Moore, *Rebellion Record*, 83, 441–42; *Chicago Times*, September 27, 1861.
8. *Chicago Times*, September 27, 1861.
9. LHS, 13, 33; *Gazetteer of McClean County*, 107; *Chicago Times*, September 26, 1861.
10. LHS, 53; *Chicago Times*, September 27, 1861.
11. LHS, 44; *Chicago Times*, September 27, 1861.
12. LHS, 44–45.
13. *Chicago Times*, September 27, 1861.
14. *St. Louis Globe-Democrat*, September 19, 1897; Anderson, *Memoirs*, 73.
15. *Chicago Times*, September 27, 1861; Moore, *Rebellion Record*, 78.
16. *SLDMR*, September 25, 1861; *Chicago Times*, September 27, 1861; Prince, *Transactions*, 144; LHS, 13, 32; Moore, *Rebellion Record*, 78; *LDH*, October 10, 1861; *Gazetteer of McClean County*, 107.
17. Luff, *Palmer Journal*, 8–9.
18. *LDH*, October 10, 1861.
19. Karamanski, *Rally Round the Flag*, 77; *Chicago Times*, September 27, 1861.

20. *SLDMR*, September 27, 1861; *Chicago Times*, September 27, 1861.

21. *HofLC*, 355; Grover, "Colonel Benjamin Whiteman Grover," 137.

22. *Chicago Times*, September 27, 1861; Love, Letters, October 10, 1861.

23. LHS, 32–33.

24. *Chicago Times*, September 27, 1861; *SLDMR*, September 27, 1861; Love, Letters, October 10, 1861; Moore, *Rebellion Record*, 83. One report said it was Captain Graham, not Major Becker, who raised the home guard's final flag of surrender.

25. *Chicago Times*, September 27, 1861; Moore, *Rebellion Record*, 73, 83; LHS, 57; *OR*, 3:187; Taylor, Narrative.

26. *Chicago Times*, September 27, 1861; Snyder, "Capture of Lexington," 4–5.

27. LHS, 57–58; Moore, *Rebellion Record*, 74; Andreas, *History of Chicago*, 192.

28. Moore, *Rebellion Record*, 74, 83; *B&L*, 313.

29. Lehr, *Deep River*, 39; Gibson, *Recollections*, 116.

30. *Chicago Times*, September 27, 1861; Coombs, *Research Report*, 30; LHS, 45; *B&L*, 313.

31. Moore, *Rebellion Record*, 76.

32. LHS, 53; Lehr, *Mockingbird*, 23; Lehr, *Deep River*, 39.

33. *Gazetteer of McClean County*, 107–08; *Chicago Times*, September 27, 1861.

34. Anderson, *Memoirs*, 74; *LDH*, October 10, 1861; *SLDMR*, September 24, 1861; Moore, *Rebellion Record*, 83.

35. Lehr, *Mockingbird*, 23; Moore, *Rebellion Record*, 74; Luff, *Palmer Journal*, 9; *HofLC*, 356; Prince, *Transactions*, 511; *Chicago Times*, September 27, 1861.

36. *OR*, 3:188; Stevens, *Centennial History*, 768; *Chicago Tribune*, October 2, 1861; *SLDMR*, October 9, 1861.

37. McHenry, Letter; Anderson, *Memoirs*, 74.

38. LHS, 33; Moore, *Rebellion Record*, 76; Snyder, "Capture of Lexington," 7.

39. Moore, *Rebellion Record*, 83.

40. Snyder, "Capture of Lexington," 6.

41. Moore, *Rebellion Record*, 76–77.

42. Tucker, Company Book; *OR*, 3:188.

43. Wyatt, "Confederate Diary," 11.

CHAPTER 10

1. Hockaday, "Letters," 54–55.

2. *NYT*, October 2, 1861.

3. Ibid.

4. Ibid.

5. Ibid.

6. Musser, "War in Missouri," 45.

7. Luff, *Palmer Journal*, 9; *CMS*, October 4, 1861.

8. *Harper's Weekly*, October 10, 1861; *HofLC*, 365; *SLDMR*, September 27, 1861.

9. *HofLC*, 356; Moore, *Rebellion Record*, 74, 76.

10. *HofLC*, 356; McCausland, "Battle of Lexington," *MHR*, 135.

11. *OR*, 3:185, 188; *CMS*, September 27, 1861; *HofLC*, 363.

12. *Cass County (MI) Republican*, October 17, 1861.

13. *Chicago Tribune*, September 26, 1861.

14. *NYT*, October 2, 1861.

15. *SLDMR*, September 24, 1861; Moore, *Rebellion Record*, 78; *Gazetteer of McClean County*, 10.

16. LHS, 33; Moore, *Rebellion Record*, 76, 83; *HofLC*, 356; Patrick, "Remembering," 48.

17. *Chicago Times*, September 27, 1861; Luff, *Palmer Journal*, 7; *Chicago Tribune*, October 4, 1861.

18. *OR*, 3:184–85; *NYT*, September 24, 26, 1861; October 10, 1861.

19. *SLDMR*, September 24, 1861; *Chicago Tribune*, October 2, 1861.

20. Moore, *Rebellion Record*, 74; White, Papers.

21. *Chicago Times*, October 5, 1861; Anderson, *Memoirs*, 76; Lehr, *Deep River*, 40.

22. *Chicago Times*, September 25, 1861; *HofLC*, 356; *Joliet (IL) Signal*, October 1, 1861; Andreas, *History of Chicago*, 193.

23. *OR*, 3:506–07; McGhee, *Memoir of Harding*, 44; Patrick, "Remembering," 49; *Gazetteer of McClean*, 108; Castel, "Siege of Lexington," 13; *SLDMR*, September 27, 1861; Banasik, *Missouri in 1861*, 197.

24. "Missouri History Not Found in Textbooks," 162; Wilkie, *Pen and Powder*, 48.

25. *HofLC*, 361; Snyder, "Capture of Lexington," 7; Lehr, *Deep River*, 40.

26. McGhee, *Memoir of Harding*, 45.

27. *OR*, 3:246–47; *NYT*, October 27, 1861; Grover, "Colonel Benjamin Whiteman Grover," 137.

28. *OR*, Series 2, 1:453–54; Moore, *Rebellion Record*, 439; Tilly, *Brilliant Success*, 49.

29. *OR*, Series 2, 4:556–61; Soldiers' Records; Banasik, *Missouri in 1861*, 185.

30. "Ordinance of Secession"; *OR*, 53:752, 758; McGhee, *Letter and Order Book*, 63.

31. Wood, *Civil War*, 76–81.

32. *OR*, 41, pt. 1:312.

33. Snyder, "Capture of Lexington," 8.

CHAPTER 11

1. Coombs, *Research Report*, 6, 29, 31; *HofLC*, 253–54; Summary of Preservation typescript.

2. *Lexington Advertiser*, October 30, 1930, "Milestone Edition."

3. *Jefferson City Daily Tribune*, July 31, 1890.

4. "Find a Grave: Machpelah Cemetery"; Fuller, E-mail.

5. "George Henry Palmer," Arlington National Cemetery website.

6. *Lexington Advertiser-News*, "Special Battle Edition," 1961; Fuller, Interview.

7. LHS.

8. McCausland, "Battle of Lexington," *MHR*, 135; Tilly, *Brilliant Success*, 55; *Lexington Advertiser-News*, September 20, 1861; Skelton, *Achieve the Honorable*, 30.

9. Haslag, "New Look," 61.

10. Farley, "Civil War Monument."

11. Gifford, *Lexington Battlefield Guide*, 25; Gueguen, "Battle of Lexington," 16.

12. Haslag, "New Look," 61; Gueguen, "Battle of Lexington," 16; Summary of Preservation typescript.

13. Coombs, *Research Report*; Gueguen, "Battle of Lexington," 16.

14. *Congressional Record*; Fuller, Interview; *Lexington Advertiser-News*, September 18–21, 1961.

15. "Battle of Lexington State Historic Site Visitor Center"; "Dedication of Union Monument in Lexington, Mo."

16. "150 Years Lexington Missouri Battle of the Hemp Bales, September 16–18, 2011"; Fuller, Interview.

17. Fuller, Interview; Battle of Lexington State Historic Site website, http://www.mostateparks.com/park/battle-lexington-state-historic-site.

BIBLIOGRAPHY

BOOKS

Anderson, Ephraim McDowell. *Memoirs: Historical and Personal; Including the Campaigns of the First Missouri Confederate Brigade.* 1868. Reprint, Dayton, OH: Press of the Morningside Bookshop, 1972.

Andreas, Alfred Theodore. *History of Chicago: From the Earliest Period to the Present Time.* Vol. 2. Chicago: A.T. Andreas Company, 1885.

Banasik, Michael E., ed. *Missouri in 1861: The Civil War Letters of Franc B. Wilkie, Newspaper Correspondent.* Iowa City, IA: Camp Pope Bookshop, 2001.

Bevier, Robert S. *History of the First and Second Missouri Confederate Brigades, 1861–1865.* St. Louis: Bryan, Brand & Company, 1879.

Britton, Wiley. *Civil War on the Border.* Vol. 1. New York: G.P. Putnam's Sons, 1899.

Burchett, Kenneth E. *The Battle of Carthage, Missouri.* Jefferson, NC: McFarland & Company, Inc., 2013.

Dyer, Frederick H. *A Compendium of the War of the Rebellion.* Des Moines, IA: Dyer Publishing Company, 1908.

Ford, S.H. *Reminiscences of S.H. Ford.* N.p., 1909. Typescript copy at State Historical Society of Missouri, Columbia.

Gazetteer of McLean County. 1866. Micro reprint in *County and Regional Histories of the "Old Northwest."* Series IV, *Illinois.* New Haven, CT: Research Publications, Inc., 1975.

Geiger, Mark W. *Financial Fraud and Guerrilla Violence in Missouri's Civil War, 1861–1865*. New Haven, CT: Yale University Press, 2010.

Gibson, J.W. *Recollections of a Pioneer*. 1912. Reprint, Independence, MO: Two Trails Publishing, 1999.

Gifford, Douglas L. *Lexington Battlefield Guide*. Winfield, MO: self-published, 2004.

Gillespie, Michael L. *The Civil War Battle of Lexington, Missouri*. Lone Jack, MO: self-published, 2007.

Grimes, Absalom Carlisle. *Confederate Mail Runner, Edited from Captain Grimes' Own Story by M.M. Quaife* New Haven, CT: Yale University Press, 1926.

Hewett, Janet B., ed. *Supplement to the Official Records of the Union and Confederate Armies*. Part 2, *Records of Events*. Vols. 37–38. Wilmington, NC: Broadfoot Publishing Co., 1996.

History of Lafayette County, Missouri, Carefully Written and Compiled from the Most Authentic Official and Private Sources, Including the History of Its Townships, Cities, Town and Villages. Warrensburg: West Central Missouri Genealogical Society and Library, Inc., 1980. Reprint, 1981.

Johnson, Robert Underwood, and Clarence Clough Buell, eds. *Battles and Leaders of the Civil War*. Vol. 1. 1887. Reprint, New York: Castle Books, 1956.

Karamanski, Theodore J. *Rally 'Round the Flag: Chicago and the Civil War*. Reprint, Lanham, MD: Rowman & Littlefield Publishers, Inc., 2006.

Lane, Peter D. *Recollections of a Volunteer: A Memoir of the Civil War*. N.p., 1865. Typescript copy at State Historical Society of Missouri, Columbia.

Lehr, Suzanne Staker, ed. *As the Mockingbird Sang: The Diary of Private Robert Caldwell Dunlap*. St. Joseph, MO: Platte Purchase Publishers, 2005.

———. *Fishing on Deep River: Civil War Memoir of Private Samuel Baldwin Dunlap, C.S.A.* St. Joseph, MO: Platte Purchase Publishers, 2006.

Lexington Historical Society, eds. *The Battle of Lexington, Fought in and around the City of Lexington, Missouri, on September 18th, 19th and 20th, 1861*. Lexington, MO: Intelligencer Printing Company, 1903.

Lexington Sesquicentennial Commemorative Book. Lexington, MO: Advance Publishing and Printing, 1972.

Luff, David A., transcriber. *The Journal of Major George H. Palmer*. Ventura, CA: self-published, 2000. Available online at http://freepages.genealogy.rootsweb.ancestry.com/~luff/PalmerGH_Journal.html.

McGhee, James E., comp. *Letter and Order Book Missouri State Guard, 1861–1862*. Independence, MO: Two Trails Publishing, 2001.

McGhee, James E., ed. *Service with the Missouri State Guard: The Memoir of Brigadier General James Harding*. Springfield, MO: Oak Hills Publishing, 2000.

McGregor, Andrew McLean. *Rambling Reminiscences of an Old Soldier during the War Between the States.* Hattiesburg, MS, 1912.

Monaghan, Jay. *Civil War on the Western Border, 1854–1865.* 1955. Reprint, Lincoln, NE: Bison Books, 1984.

Moore, Frank, ed. *The Rebellion Record: A Diary of American Events.* Vol. 3. 1862. Reprint, New York: Arno Press, 1977.

Past and Present of Rock Island County, Illinois. Chicago: H.F. Kett and Company, 1877.

Prince, Ezra Morton, ed. *Transactions of the McLean County Historical Society.* Vol. 1. Bloomington, IL: Pantagraph Printing and Stationery Company, 1899.

Skelton, Ike. *Achieve the Honorable: A Missouri Congressman's Journey from Warm Springs to Washington.* Carbondale: Southern Illinois University Press, 2013.

Snead, Thomas I. *The Fight for Missouri: From the Election of Lincoln to the Death of Lyon.* New York: Charles Scribner's Sons, 1888.

Stevens, Walter Barlow. *Centennial History of Missouri (the Center State): One Hundred Years in the Union, 1820–1921.* Vol. 1. St. Louis: S.J. Clarke Publishing Company, 1921.

Tilly, Kevin I. *Brilliant Success in Missouri: Sterling Price's Patriot Army and the 1861 Campaign for Lexington.* Blue Springs, MO: self-published, 2008.

Vivian, Martha Campbell. *Down the Avenue of Ninety Years.* N.p.: self-published, 1924.

The War of the Rebellion: A Compilation of the Official Records of the Union and Confederate Armies. Washington, D.C.: Government Printing Office, 1880–1901. Available online at http://ebooks.library.cornell.edu/m/moawar/waro.html.

Wilkie, Franc B. *Pen and Powder.* Boston: Ticknor and Company, 1888.

Wood, Larry. *Civil War Springfield.* Charleston, SC: The History Press, 2011.

ARTICLES

Armstrong, Robert. "Other Side in Battle of Lexington, Mo." *Confederate Veteran* 20 (1912): 467–68.

"Battle of Lexington State Historic Site Visitor Center." *Civil War Muse.* http://www.thecivilwarmuse.com/index.php?page=battle-of-lexington-state-historic-site-visitor-center.

Castel, Albert. "The Siege of Lexington." *Civil War Times Illustrated* 8 (August 1969): 4–13.

Bibliography

"Dedication of Union Monument in Lexington, Mo." *Authentic Campaigner*. http://www.authentic-campaigner.com/forum/showthread.php?24400-Dedication-of-Union-monument-in-Lexington-Mo.

Farley, Kevin. "Civil War Monument Re-Dedicated on Wentworth Campus." http://www.wma.edu/civil-war-monument-re-dedicated-on-wentworth-campus.

"Find a Grave: Machpelah Cemetery." http://www.findagrave.com/php/famous.php?page=cem&FScemeteryid=466267.

Grover, George S. "Colonel Benjamin Whiteman Grover." *Missouri Historical Review* 1 (January 1907): 129–39.

Gueguen, John A., Jr. "The Battle of Lexington Sept. 18, 19, 20, 1861." In *Lexington Sesquicentennial Commemorative Book*. Lexington, MO: Advance Publishing and Printing, 1972.

Haslag, Leonard F. "A New Look at the Anderson House and the Civil War Battle of Lexington State Park." *Missouri Historical Review* 56 (October 1961): 59–68.

Hockaday, Isaac. "Letters from the Battle of Lexington: 1861." *Missouri Historical Review* 56 (October 1961): 53–58.

Hyde, William S. "Dear Sister," September 16, 1861, and "Dear Mother," September 25, 1861, in *Lexington Intelligencer*, March 8, 1902.

Mansur, W.H. "Incident of the Battle of Lexington, Mo." *Confederate Veteran* 23 (January 1915): 496.

"May 10, 1861: The Capture of Camp Jackson in St. Louis." Missouri Civil War Museum website. http://www.mcwm.org/history_camp_jackson.html.

McCausland, Susan A. Arnold. "The Battle of Lexington as Seen by a Woman." *Missouri Historical Review* 6 (January 1912): 127–35.

McCausland, Susan Arnold. "The Battle of Lexington." *Confederate Veteran* 20 (1912): 223–26.

McDonald, William N. "Capture of Lexington, Missouri, by Price's Army." *Southern Bivouac* 3 (November 1884): 105–10.

"Missouri History: Geographical Distribution of Slavery." www.missouri-history.itgo.com/slave.html.

"Missouri History Not Found in Textbooks." *Missouri Historical Review* 35 (October 1940): 162.

Morton, Charles. "Early War Days in Missouri." In *Papers Read Before the Commandery of the State of Wisconsin, Military Order of the Loyal Legion of the United States*. Vol. 2. Milwaukee: Burdick, Armitage & Allen, 1896: 145–58.

Musser, Richard H. "The War in Missouri." Parts 2 and 3. *Southern Bivouac* 4 (May 1886): 745–52; 5 (June 1886): 43–48.

Nixon, Oliver W. "Reminiscences of the First Year of the War in Missouri." In *Military Essays and Recollections: Papers Read Before the Commandery of the State of Illinois, Military Order of the Loyal Legion of the United States*. Vol. 3. Chicago: Dial Press, 1899: 413–36.

"150 Years Lexington Missouri Battle of the Hemp Bales September 16–18, 2011." http://mostateparks.com/sites/default/files/reenactorinfo.pdf.

Patrick, Jeffrey L. "The Battle of Lexington." *North & South* 1 (February 1998): 52–67.

Patrick, Jeffrey L., ed. "Remembering the Missouri Campaign of 1861: The Memoirs of Lt. William Barlow, Guibor's Battery, Missouri State Guard." *Civil War Regiments* 5 (1997): 20–60.

Smith, Harold F. "Mulligan and the Irish Brigade." *Journal of the Illinois State Historical Society* 56 (1963): 164–76.

Snyder, J.F. "The Capture of Lexington." *Missouri Historical Review* 7 (October, 1912): 1–9.

Williams, Scott. "The Role of German Immigrants in Civil War Missouri." Missouri Civil War Museum, St. Louis. www.mcwm.org/history-germans.html.

Winter, William C., ed. "'Amidst Trials and Troubles': Captain Samuel Churchill Clark, C.S.A." *Missouri Historical Review* 92 (October 1977): 1–17.

Wyatt, John. "A Confederate Diary." *White River Valley Historical Quarterly* 36, no. 3 (Winter 1997): 8–15.

PUBLIC DOCUMENTS AND UNPUBLISHED SOURCES

Battle of Lexington State Historic Site website. http://www.mostateparks.com/park/battle-lexington-state-historic-site.

Benton, Richard Higgins. "The Autobiography of Richard Higgins Benton" (C0995). Typescript. State Historical Society of Missouri Manuscript Collection, Columbia.

Brown, Richard. Narrative. Battle of Lexington State Historic Site Collection.

Carter, R. Creed. "A Short Sketch of My Experiences during the First Stages of the War" (C2911). State Historical Society of Missouri Manuscript Collection, Columbia.

Congressional Record—House. September 1961. http://www.mocavo.com/Congressional-Record-Volume-107-8/763065/566.

Coombs, Kenneth E. *Research Report: Restoration and Development, Civil War Battle of Lexington State Park, Lexington, Missouri.* Prepared for the Missouri State Park Board, Jefferson City, MO, 1961.

Eighth Population Census of the United States—1860. http://www.joplinpubliclibrary.org/reference/ref_genealogy.php.

Fuller, Janae. E-mail message, January 15, 2014.

———. Interview, January 14, 2014.

"George Henry Palmer." Arlington National Cemetery Website. http://www.arlingtoncemetery.net/ghpalmer.htm.

"Haerle Family History." Typescript. Battle of Lexington State Historic Site Collection, Lexington, Missouri.

Illinois Civil War Muster and Descriptive Rolls. Illinois State Archives, Springfield, Illinois. http://www.cyberdriveillinois.com/departments/archives/databases/datcivil.html.

Keith, Thomas J. Journal (B295). Missouri Historical Museum, St. Louis.

Love, James E. Civil War Love Letters. Missouri Historical Museum, St. Louis. http://www.historyhappenshere.org/archives/category/love-letters.

Maki, John. Interview, November 25, 2013.

McHenry, Eli Bass. Letter, October 1, 1901. Typescript copy in the collection of James McGhee.

McNamara, J.H. "An Historical Sketch of the Sixth Division, Missouri State Guard." In Mosby Monroe Parsons Papers (A309). Missouri Historical Museum, St. Louis.

The Oliver Anderson House. Leaflet. Jefferson City: Missouri Department of Natural Resources, 1998.

"Ordinance of Secession." Trans-Mississippi Theater Virtual Museum. http://www.civilwarvirtualmuseum.org/1861-1862/12th-confederate-state/ordinance-of-secession.php.

Sitton, John James. Memoir. Typescript (R377). State Historical Society of Missouri Manuscript Collection, Rolla.

Smith, I.V. Personal Memoirs, April 1902 (C705). State Historical Society of Missouri Manuscript Collection, Columbia.

Soldiers' Records: War of 1812–World War I. Missouri State Archives, Jefferson City. http://www.sos.mo.gov/archives/resources/resources.asp.

Summary of Preservation. Typescript. Battle of Lexington State Historic Site Collection.

Taylor, John. Narrative. Battle of Lexington State Historic Site Collection.

Thomas, John A., and Susan McMahon Thomas. Letters, 1861. Typescripts. Missouri State Archives, Jefferson City.

Tucker, James J. Company Book, Company E, Clarkson's Regiment, Missouri State Guard. Collection of the Hulston Library, Wilson's Creek National Battlefield, Republic, MO.

White, Robert. Papers (B648). Missouri Historical Museum, St. Louis. http://collections.mohistory.org.

NEWSPAPERS

Cass County (MI) Republican
Chicago Times
Chicago Tribune
Columbia Missouri Statesman
Higginsville (MO) Advance
Jefferson City Daily Tribune
Joliet (IL) Signal
Lexington (MO) Advertiser
Lexington (MO) Advertiser-News
Lexington (MO) Intelligencer
Liberty (MO) Tribune
Louisiana (MO) Democratic Herald
New York Times
St. Louis Daily Missouri Republican
St. Louis Globe-Democrat
Staunton (VA) Spectator
White Cloud Kansas Chief

INDEX

Index

INDEX

ABOUT THE AUTHOR

Larry Wood is a retired public school teacher and freelance writer specializing in the history of the Ozarks and surrounding region. He has published two historical novels, ten nonfiction history books, and numerous magazine stories and articles. His previous books for The History Press include *The Two Civil War Battles of Newtonia* and *Civil War Springfield*. He and his wife, Gigi, live in Joplin, Missouri.

Visit us at
www.historypress.net

· ·

This title is also available as an e-book